Mathematical Learning Difficulties
in the Secondary School

Mathematical Learning Difficulties in the Secondary School

Pupil Needs and Teacher Roles

ANTONY LARCOMBE

OPEN UNIVERSITY PRESS

Milton Keynes · Philadelphia

Open University Press
12 Cofferidge Close
Stony Stratford
Milton Keynes MK11 1BY. England
and
242 Cherry Street
Philadelphia, PA 19106, USA

First Published 1985

British Library Cataloguing in Publication Data

Larcombe, Antony
  Mathematical learning difficulties in the secondary school:
  pupil needs and teacher roles.
  1. Mathematics—Study and teaching (Secondary)
  I. Title
  510′7′12   QA11

  ISBN 0–335–15020–9

Library of Congress Cataloging in Publication Data

Larcombe, Anthony.
  Mathematical learning difficulties in the secondary school.
    Bibliography: p. 112
    Includes index.
    1. Mathematics—Study and teaching (Secondary)
  2. Learning disabilities.   I. Title.
  QA11.L378   1985   510′.7′12   84–22815
  ISBN 0–335–15020–9 (pbk.)

Text design by Nicola Sheldon

Typeset by Freeman Graphic, Tonbridge, Kent.
Printed in Great Britain by St. Edmundsbury Press,
Bury St. Edmunds, Suffolk.

Contents

Introduction

There is nothing more difficult to take in hand, more perilous to conduct, or more uncertain in its success, than to take the lead in the introduction of a new order of things, because the innovator has for enemies all those who have done well under the old conditions. Machiavelli 'The Prince'.

These words from Machiavelli seem to ring so true for those of us who have tried to raise issues and challenge assumptions on behalf of pupils generally accepted as inevitable failures within the school system. We have become used to reading, in descriptions of published mathematics courses, such statements as 'this course is not intended to meet the needs of the bottom 25%'. We accept with our ears and our minds that the CSE examination was not intended to reach down below the least able 40% in the population. Yet almost all the pupils below that mark are pushed into a CSE course, and the 'non-examination pupil' is a rare and often hopeless exception within the system. We do have extensive provision for the last able in mathematics in the first two or three years in our secondary schools, but why is this provision not continued?

Can we find hope for radical change to this sort of situation, from the Cockcroft Report?[1] It does seem so clearly and positively to highlight the problems for the pupils, draws attention to the spread of ability with which we have to deal and takes such a timely look at the nature of mathematics learning and the place of mathematics in society. Perhaps we should take great encouragement from

1

statements like: '... development should be from "the bottom upwards" by considering the range of work which is appropriate for lower-attaining pupils'. Yet what does that really mean or in what ways is it understood?

There does seem, to be a great danger of everybody saying 'Yes, yes, yes' to the statements in such a document. Each person involved finds justification and support for their own position and yet no real change occurs.

In this contribution to the general discussion about mathematics learning I adopt the stand-point (advocated by Warnock[2]) that we should plan the curriculum with a careful eye to the special needs of our pupils. Broadly I argue that the pattern of provision for mathematics education for the low attaining pupil should be at least as much influenced by our recognition and understanding of that pupil's needs as it is by our view of what mathematics should be taught at any given stage.

I argue that the most significant thing brought to the mathematics lesson by the pupil is a set of feelings and attitudes towards mathematics. In short, the key task for the teacher of the low attainer is to replace in the learner a syndrome of reinforced failure by the recognition of success and achievement in mathematics which will motivate and generate an interest in learning the subject. I begin, therefore, with pupils' feelings and attitudes and the effect on them of school practices in mathematics. I go on to re-examine what is really significant about mathematics and mathematics learning for pupils who have serious difficulties with the subject. Finally, I develop a rationale for effective classroom practice. During the course of this journey I make detailed explorations of failure, worth and motivation; of concept development, problem-solving and assessment; and of *how* as well as why, particularly with regard to the special needs of older pupils.

The whole is put forward, not as a definitive answer or a blue print to be copied, but as an awareness-raising discussion which will bring into focus a wide range of issues for the reader. I do believe that one of the greatest problems schools face is that, for one reason or another, such issues are not raised or cannot be discussed.

I have chosen to illustrate my argument with examples from an individualized learning approach (rather than from thematic or modular approaches). I have not chosen this model because I believe it to be the only model that might be used to meet the individual needs of pupils but becuase it does seem the most appropriate with which to illuminate the earlier discussion in the book. Throughout the book I have used Boxes. In these I have included case material anecdotes and other detail which put flesh on the skeleton of my arguments.

one

The Background of Feelings and Attitudes

When Phoebe burst out with the comment ''he thinks we enjoy playin' all these games. I want to do real maths!', it was the source of considerable embarrassment for me, a mere visitor to her fourth year secondary class. The major source of my embarrassment was not the content of her comment nor really that she sounded and indeed looked indignant when she made it, but simply that the teacher of whom she spoke so scornfully, was seated with a group of pupils no more than two metres away.

It would of course be naive and facile to take the comments and frustrations of a single pupil and generalize from them a whole view of the problems of pupils with difficulty in learning mathematics. At the same time it would be foolish to disregard the issues raised by her comments, especially since I suspect she was simply articulate enough and perhaps brave enough to put into words what many other pupils might well say.

Three key points seem to be highlighted by her comment which I would identify thus:

(i) Pupils do have feelings about the learning situation in which they find themselves.
(ii) Pupils do have their own way of perceiving what they believe mathematics to be.
(iii) Pupils anticipate and expect that the teacher will have a motive behind the planning of the work for the learner.

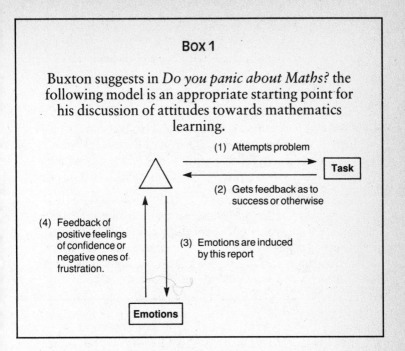

Box 1

Buxton suggests in *Do you panic about Maths?* the following model is an appropriate starting point for his discussion of attitudes towards mathematics learning.

(1) Attempts problem

Task

(2) Gets feedback as to success or otherwise

(4) Feedback of positive feelings of confidence or negative ones of frustration.

(3) Emotions are induced by this report

Emotions

Such factors as these are, I believe, likely to be bound up with others to form what I shall call an 'affective filter' through which the pupil sees mathematics in school.

It is all too easy in a discussion on mathematics to be drawn into descriptions of content and approaches to teaching and learning the subject, as though that was the starting point. I believe, however, that any discussion about mathematics learning with pupils who display difficulty in the subject must commence with a very deliberate look at what might be going on in the mind of the learner.

Laurie Buxton[3] (see Box 1) and others have highlighted connections between feelings and mathematics in such a way that we cannot escape the fact that there must be great implications for those who seek to teach the subject. Whether or not that which applies to mathematics applies also to other subjects or whether mathematics is in some way unique is not a question for discussion here. What seems essential, however, is to consider first under what conditions and with what consequences the affective filtering becomes critical in the

---

Box 2

In the course of observation and enquiry into the classroom mathematics work of disaffected adolescents, which I was carrying out, I developed the habit of very direct questioning. This technique was only used after a good rapport had been established and often included the injuction 'Tell me about the time when you used to enjoy doing maths at school'.

To my great surprise in over thirty cases where this particular 'challenge' was thrown out only once did it evoke the response 'I never did like maths'. In about every other case, often without even a pause for thought, a warm description flowed. Frequently it went way back to the infant school.

---

learning of mathematics for some pupils, and secondly whether the negative effects of this filtering can be reduced or even if the onset of such filtering can be avoided.

Evidence of negative feelings and attitudes to mathematics learning is so common a factor amongst the least able pupils in our secondary schools that we are in great danger of assuming that it will inevitably be present. We are in danger of planning our work against the assumption that it is just a factor with which we have to live. In many classrooms however this is demonstrably not the case: pupils are learning mathematics in a co-operative, purposeful way where they are developing very positive attitudes towards the work. But such classrooms seem strangely few and far between. yet, when listening to teachers of the least able, it is so easy to find support for the comment 'It is not teaching the mathematics that takes up my time so much as dealing with all the other problems.'

I do not believe it is easy to separate out 'the other things' from the mathematics. Indeed Rutter[4] suggests that disaffected behaviour is more commonly the outcome of educational failure than the cause of it. In my own enquiries amongst older secondary pupils (Box 2) it seemed clear that for many maths-hating pupils the dislike for mathematics had not always existed. I believe that the development of this dislike is greatly bound up with knowledge of, and fear of failure. Part, if you like, of a syndrome of reinforced failure whose most marked effect is upon the pupils' motivation towards mathematics learning.

It would seem unlikely that pupils who perceive themselves as failures develop that view with respect to one school subject to the exclusion of any other just because of the nature of the content. Nevertheless, many pupils do feel themselves to be particular failures in mathematics. I suspect this is more to do with the way in which pupils are required to work in mathematics in school than anything inherent in the subject itself.

The work of many psychologists, including Maslow[5] highlights the deep psychological need for esteem. He argues that achievement and recognition are key factors in the development of this esteem. In mathematics achievement is usually clear since answers are often simply right or wrong; but recognition will depend upon the way that the teacher responds to the work the pupil has done. Whether teacher feedback is positive (thus enhancing a pupil's self esteem and esteem in the eyes of others) or negative, may not matter in isolated instances. When, however, it becomes a regular pattern then great significance must be attached to it. Repeated positive reinforcement must lead to building of esteem, repeated negative reinforcement quite the opposite. The tragic truth is that those pupils who, by whatever arrangement or with whatever titles or euphemisms we may describe them in school, have developed a syndrome of reinforced failure in *mathematics* are likely to become generally disadvantaged pupils before very long.

Downward spiralling of self esteem is so easily the seeding ground for self fulfilling prophecies, and both pupil and teacher can get to the point where – on the basis of previous failure – they cannot even anticipate that success might be an outcome of future work.

At this point it seems reasonable to assume that motivation is likely to have broken down completely. Particularly if we take note of Maslow's suggestion that 'Everyone needs to feel that he is making reasonable progress towards a manageable goal.'

Perhaps we should stop at this point and ask if this downward spiral could have been averted. Suppose we ask analytical questions like:

'Why was this pupil given work which in the first place led to considerable errors?'

'Why did the finding of errors have to be delayed until the end of the work or if the errors were in evidence during the work why did the teacher not intervene to help the pupil over them?'

'Why did the pupil move on to further work which led to errors rather than being given the opportunity to achieve mastery at one level before moving on?'

It is interesting to note how it has become commonly accepted that pupils may well be at different stages of development of language and communicative skills and that therefore the significant factor in choosing books suitable is reading age rather than chronological age. In mathematics, however, we see pupils in most schools being given work to do on the basis of year group rather than on their mathematical stage of development. There seems to be wide acceptance for the tendency of publishers to describe suitability of the content of mathematics texts by reference to the year group for whom the work is designed. In the rare cases where *the level of mathematics development* is described teachers are often quite hesitant in using the material. This is the more surprising given that Cockcroft[6] highlighted that a 'seven year' spread of mathematics ability could be anticipated at the First Year stage in the Secondary School. Perhaps in the light of Cockcroft one vital response might be attempts made to publish more material which sets out to provide for such a range of ability at a given age but unless this is matched by a willingness to cater for spread in the classroom it will be to no avail. It is puzzling to find that within the Cockcroft Report itself the same authors who emphasize the

---

Box 3

From I. M. Hulicka in Roucek, J. S. (ed.), *The Slow Learner*.

In direct academic competition with the 'advantaged' child the 'disadvantaged' child may be doomed to failure, and repeated failures may contribute to a change in motivational emphasis which may in turn increase the experiential gap between the 'disadvantaged' and the 'advantaged' child. the probability that the teacher will be able to help the 'disadvantaged' child overcome experiential handicaps in the academic sphere will be greater if he structures academic experiences so that the 'disadvantaged' child is rewarded for what he knows rather than punished or humiliated for what he is or doesn't know.

---

spread take such a guarded stance over the emerging individualized learning schemes such as SMILE[7] and KMP[8], which are specifically designed with the spread in mind.

It is not only the problems of achievement which are exacerbated by planning work according to age or year group but also the problem of recognition. Where 'year group' development is the focus or reference point for pupils' progress then it is almost inevitable that a rank ordering of pupils will exist either informally in the minds of the teachers or formally in the documents and lists passed around the school. In so many secondary schools there will even be end of term/year exams designed to produce a rank order which makes formal recognition of the relative 'failure' of the pupils in the lower part of the rank order. Hulicka[9] argues (Box 3) the overriding need for teachers to give recognition to the competencies rather than to the incompetencies of pupils if we are to improve motivation.

Another factor which bears some influence on the relationship between success and motivation is the whole notion of 'worth'. This is arguably the aspect most likely to change over time as motivation, social and emotional development

---

Box 4

It has been my experience in visiting the least able pupils in a large number of schools that more often than not one is taken out of the main part of the school into an 'environmentally undesirable' part of the establishment where these pupils will be found working. In one school, admittedly an extreme, this meant walking out of the buildings across a playground, onto a path between playing fields, across a bridge over the river, and into a corner of the fields where a mobile classroom housed the 'remedial department'.

In one primary school each year group had a 'slow moving' class. The rest of the school was housed in spacious modern buildings but there were four mobile classrooms clustered in the far corner of the playground. This housed the four 'slow moving' classes. The head explained 'We find having them together helps provide the pupils with an identity and a sense of security'.

---

will all influence the pupil's perception of what mathematics achievement is 'worth'. For some pupils at certain stages their notion of the worth of mathematics may simply reflect *teacher* attitudes. At other stages *peer* attitudes may be more significant and, particularly at the later stage of the secondary school, the perception of worth may be bound up with ideas of examinations and employment prospects. In the case of young slow learners Williams[10] suggests that the *parental* attitude towards education is of very considerable significance in the pupil's view of worth.

the reflection of teacher attitudes is most obvious when pupils make unquestioning responses to teacher 'rules' and 'procedures' for presenting work. But teacher attitudes are conveyed, read, and reflected back not only by procedures but also in 'body language' communicated by the range of

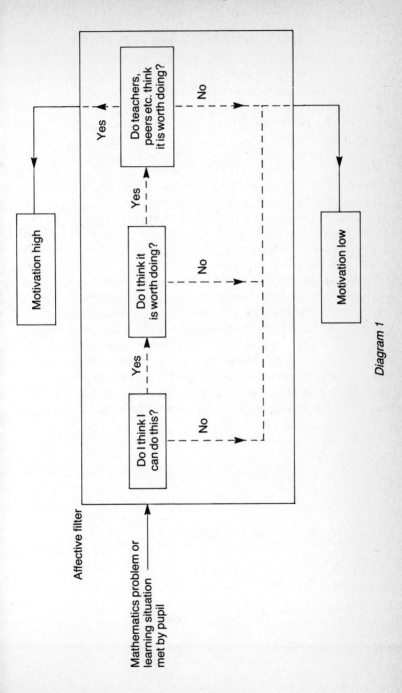

Diagram 1

facial expressions, gestures, postures and inflections in the voice of teachers, even in the use of humour or sarcasm. Pupils also recognize indicators of the worth of mathematics in the wider school environment. These indicators may range from the choice of rooms (see Box 4) to the timetabling and staffing provision for the least able or even the provision and condition of apparatus.

Mathematics, which is currently short of specialist teachers is, in my experience, particularly prone to *ad hoc* staffing for the 'bottom sets' in ordinary schools. It is not very difficult to find teachers who were not trained – and had never intended to teach the subject – involved in mathematics with the least able pupils. Certainly some teachers have made an unqualified success in adapting to this changed role but many see it as only a temporary expedient which is neither desirable nor enjoyable. In certain cases I have seen very low ability pupils whose mathematics lessons are shared between as many as three different non-specialist teachers. The pupils draw their own conclusions about the status and worth of mathematics so do the staff. It is no wonder that in many schools those who work with the least able appear to have developed the impression that they are considered low grade teachers.

These notions of failure, motivation, and worth are related in Diagram 1. The implications of the model are discussed in the next two chapters.

two

Failure and Motivation

If a reinforced pattern of failure is the greatest threat to pupil esteem and undermines the whole attempt to educate the pupil mathematically, we must examine closely the implications of this for the curriculum.

It cannot be enough to say that in place of negative reinforcement we must put positive reinforcement. First we must identify at what points negative reinforcement can arise and then develop possible strategies to overcome it. I shall identify what I believe are some of the principal 'weak points' but this is not to suggest that each exists in every school or in the experience of every pupil. Nevertheless, each school does need to identify aspects of its organization and practice which might be considered its own 'weak points'.

In my own very general list I offer these:

1. Choice of work does not match mathematical level of pupil.
2. Teaching style does not match individual needs of the pupil.
3. Incorrect assumptions about the strengths and weaknesses of individual pupils.
4. Choice of current and subsequent pieces of work does not relate to past success or failure.
5. Teaching materials are not suited to the needs of the pupil.
6. School assessments are in conflict with a teaching model based upon meeting needs of pupils.

Let us then look more closely at each of these:

1. Choice of work does not match mathematical level of pupil

Underlying all that has been said so far, and will subsequently be said, is the assumption that the mathematical development of each pupil is highly individual. Whilst there will be a degree of overlap between pupils we cannot assume common starting points or identical patterns of concept development or understanding. In addition to this the rate at which pupils learn will vary so that we would expect them to progress to quite different points and by implication the longer the schooling process has gone on then the further apart these points will be. Certainly Cockcroft highlights this at 11+ and argues the need for a differentiated curriculum in mathematics.

If we are to accept this as an argument then surely there is a great need to recognize it in practice as we plan work for pupils who will be critically affected if what is given to them is of quite the wrong order of difficulty. There is a need then to identify what pupils are able to do and understand and use this as the starting point for our work. Gulliford[11] argues the case for early identification of pupils' needs for various reasons including 'the development of teaching procedures' to meet needs.

It is all too common to find tests and other diagnostic procedures used in mathematics to discover what the pupil cannot do. This is often followed by concentrated teaching designed to put this right. When looking at a pupil's progress in school over some years it may well be the case that year after year the same inability has been identified and 'hammered' time and time again. This can only confirm pupil and teacher alike in the view that so and so cannot 'do' fractions or whatever. How much more appropriate as Maurice Chazan[12] argues to build up a picture of what the pupil *can* do at this stage (see Box 5). The next requirement is to ensure that what we ask the pupil to do is realistic and manageable in the light of what we discover.

Box 5

This excerpt is taken from Chazan's contribution to Wedell, K. and Raybould, E. C., 'The early Identification of Educationally 'at risk' Children'.

Maurice Chazan draws attention to the dangers of early identification of pupils' learning and other difficulties. Pupils are labelled early which leads to treatment according to label rather than treatment according to needs.

He argues that on balance 'if we can prevent early poor adjustment from becoming fixed then it is worth taking the risks accompanying early identification of problems'.

'We must ensure that we never look at a child in wholly negative terms.' To avoid this he suggests 'all screening procedures should include questions of a positive nature as well as those asking for indications of poor adjustment'.

Seen in this way our planning of pupil work will be such that the progression of the work is a response to the needs of the pupils. The mathematics, although carefully guided by teachers, will unfold in relation to individual pupil need rather than following a pre-planned mathematical pathway down which we try to direct *all* the pupils at a predetermined rate.

Each pupil is at a different starting point. That surely is why those who have sought to make pupil needs the main determinant of how to plan mathematics work have ended up with some sort of individualized approach. (Conversely it is why some abandon hope of meeting individual needs because they argue – 'You cannot plan for each pupil separately.')

However, responding to needs is not of concern only at the start of our work with a particular pupil but should continue to be a guiding principle. This requires monitoring of progress and record keeping to ensure that we maintain a close match between need, achievement and the level of demands we place on the pupil.

2. Teaching style does not match individual needs of the pupil

Cockcroft suggests that the teaching of mathematics to all pupils should include opportunities for:

1. Exposition by the teacher;
2. Discussion between teacher and pupil and between pupils themselves;
3. Appropriate practical work;
4. Consolidation and practice of fundamental skills and routines;
5. Problem solving, including the application of mathematics to everyday situations;
6. Investigational work.

There is a need, however, to consider which teaching style might be appropriate and for which pupils at what stage. The most valuable asset in the classroom, it is so often agreed, is the teacher. Of course teachers are valuable but in practice, with the day to day pressures and responsibilities of the classroom, how flexible are they?

Should there be one teaching style per whole lesson, even for every lesson, for all the pupils or should the teacher promote several or even, on some occasions, all of these activities in a single lesson! Historically we have seen classroom transactions rooted in the lecture or demonstration mode where every pupil gives attention to the teacher at the same time. If, however, pupils are at different stages in their work, even doing quite dissimilar things this model becomes inappropriate. A great deal of negative criticism is currently being directed at the use of workcards in mathematics. Many of the critics suggest that workcards will never achieve what can be achieved by exposition. Others suggest the use of workcards tends to isolate pupils and removes the opportunity for discussion or that they discourage teachers from entering into dialogue with the pupil. Surely the argument is not whether we use either the teacher or the workcard but rather how can we make better use of both to ensure a wider range of methods of working with our pupils.

Many teachers would argue that the use of workcards has enabled them to create a dialogue with one or two pupils whilst the rest are engaged in their own work. Exposition can happen alongside the workcards but to a selected audience from within the group. Carefully planned workcards can become the means of drawing together a group of pupils to discuss the mathematics. A group of pupils can gather at the overhead projector or the blackboard whilst others are engaged with their apparatus elsewhere in the room.

Surely what matters in choosing teaching style (as much as in choosing mathematical content) is that the way of working we choose for this pupil at this stage enables us to meet the pupil's needs effectively, recognizing that for this pupil the requirement might change shortly. A programme of mathematics work which depends upon the use of only one style of working – and that for all pupils – is bound to be 'reaching' fewer pupils than a programme which can call on a range of styles and approaches. In classrooms where individualized schemes in mathematics are used to best effect it is a feature of the work that the teacher is integrating the use of the workcards with investigation work, with group teaching, exposition etc.

A further consideration is the interruption to learning through absence. Where all the teaching input is focused on the teacher's activity in the classroom it becomes increasingly difficult to compensate for absence of the pupil. For instance, some teachers use a modular approach with a key 'starter' lesson presented to the whole group after which varied activity flows, for perhaps the next two or three weeks, with pupils pursuing the topic in different ways. Clearly absence by a pupil from the key lesson will affeect quite drastically the value of the 'follow up' work. If absence is a regular occurrence for a particular pupil, as is so often the case from the middle years in the secondary school, both the modular and the class teaching approach will become very vulnerable.

Box 6

Holt observes in *How Children Fail* . . .

'Success implies overcoming an obstacle, including, perhaps the thought in our minds that we might not succeed. It is turning "I can't" into "I can and did".'

---

3. Incorrect assumptions about the strengths and weaknesses of individual pupils

All that has been highlighted in the previous two sections could be carefully attended to and a really considered response to the perceived needs of the pupils made, but still the teacher may have developed a mistaken view of what a pupil's mathematical strengths and weaknesses are. In addition to this pupils' understanding and attitudes towards mathematics will be changing over time, so it is easy to make assumptions which become out of date.

It is not surprising that there is great concern about 'labelling' pupils. The most obvious danger is of inadvertently ensuring that pupils remain at a 'low level' simply by underestimating their level. John Holt[13] notes that it is common to find perceptions of success on the part of the pupils linked with meeting *new* learning as distinct from repeating things already known and understood (Box 6). Yet so often when we think of giving pupils the opportunity to 'demonstrate success' we are tempted to present them with things we believe they already know. In my experience motivation can break down just as easily if a pupil is repeatedly 'under challenged' as it can if the pupil is 'over challenged'.

A second danger area for making assumptions exists in the way we observe the outcomes of a pupil's learning. Traditionally we have come to look for written proof of understanding and yet, particularly with younger less able pupils,

---

Box 7

Holt recalls this anecdote in *How Children Fail*

The other day I was working with a sixteen year old boy who was having trouble with first year physics. I asked him to do one of the problems in his book. Immediately he began to write on his paper 'Given', then, under it, 'To Find' and under that 'Use'. He began to fill in the spaces with a hash of letters and figures. I said, 'Whoa, hold on, at least think about it before you start writing down a mess of stuff.' He said, 'But our teacher tells us we have to do all our problems this way.'

So there we are. No doubt this teacher would say that he wants his students to think about problems, and that he prescribed this form so that they would think. But what he has not seen, and probably never will see, is that his means to the end of clear thinking has become an end in itself, just part of the ritual mumbo-jumbo you have to go through on your answer hunt.

---

and in fact many who are not less able, the ability to communicate in an abstract symbolic and written form is likely to be nowhere near as highly developed as the mathematical understanding. How erroneous our judgements can be if we base them only on what the pupil is able to write down. At certain stages in the development of any concept there may well be points at which we need to hear the pupil talking about the mathematics as they see it if we are ever to gain access to the way they are thinking. There is also the converse problem where it may well look, from what is written, as though a pupil understands just because the right answer is there. In fact, I suspect there are many pupils who see learning mathematics only in terms of an effort towards writing correct answers. (See Box 7)

A further danger is that of supposing that the pupil who has problems in learning in one aspect of mathematics will therefore find all mathematics equally difficult. Certainly some will have general problems throughout the field of mathematics but there are so many exceptions. These exceptions quite commonly include those youngsters with genuine problems over most number work but who have little or no problem over transactions involving money; those who have remarkably well developed spatial awareness but who find number related work difficult; those who have severe psycho-motor problems which make for exceptional difficulty with drawing related work but have no problem with numbers. The list could be extensive.

Yet another danger with pupils with severe reading problems is that of assuming that mathematical inactivity is due to severe conceptual problems in mathematics when in fact it is difficult for the pupil to gain access to the mathematics because of the language problem.

It would be easy to labour the point by extending the list of dangerous areas for making assumptions but it cannot be over-stated that it is all too easy to make careful and well-meaning attempts at informed assessments of pupils' needs but end up producing an inadequate and limiting framework of assumptions which lock the pupil into inevitable failure. How careful we must be to develop the habit of continually challenging, questioning and updating our assumptions as we monitor the progress of the pupils. However, on balance it must be preferable to find teachers risking the dangers and looking for insights into the pupil rather than using the dangers as a reason or excuse to ignore the problem completely.

4. Choice of current and subsequent pieces of work does not relate to past success or failure

If we subscribe to a developmental view of concept formation in mathematics then clearly we will plan to provide some sort of continuity to the mathematics programme. The closer the plan matches the actual development of the particular pupil then presumably the more effective we shall be in providing

---

Box 8

The following are comments gleaned from teacher discussions at the Primary/Secondary Interface.

... 'We don't like to feel prejudiced about the pupils who come to us so we make it a practice to withhold showing the primary records to the first year teachers until the first few months have elapsed.'

... 'There is no point in looking in too much detail because our First Year timetable and syllabus is all fixed before they come to us.'

... 'The records are not a lot of help because our pupils come from so many different schools you just can't compare them.'

... 'The Secondary School we feed come down to consult with us in July over the problem children. They even lend us books and suggest the work that will help the pupils become familiar with the sort of work they will do.'

---

the experiences the pupil needs and in increasing the opportunities for the pupil to enjoy successful work. However, we must be aware that there are particular points at which forward planning is liable to constitute a real problem. If, for example, the programme is beginning, for one reason or another, to become less effective and the anticipated progress and success do not occur, it is easy to press on regardless in the hope that we shall soon 'turn a corner'. In fact, we may well have been wiser to plan with a much shorter time span in mind so that cutting our losses and changing strategy would have been easier. The converse can also be a problem when the pupil begins to demonstrate success in an area where hitherto progress has been very slow and painstaking: then it can sometimes be difficult to modify one's view of what a pupil can achieve and work to more ambitious targets. Many teachers speak of the stage when a particular pupil appears to have 'taken off' with his or her work.

Another stage when continuity is at risk is the stage when, at the onset of a new school year, pupils will move into the care of the next teacher, a problem which is particularly pronounced when this entails a change of school. Traditionally the notion of what pupils 'ought' to be able to do at a particular stage tends to influence what is done far more than comments and evidence passed on by the previous teacher. The hard work for increase in confidence and self esteem which has developed over years can be broken down in the first few days in the new school or class. (See Box 8)

Major change can also arise when a pupil moves away from remedial support back into the mainstream work of the school. Again this is a single move which can destroy, in this case in the course of days, the confidence which has been built up over months. A great deal of care, preparation and planning must be taken over such moves.

5. Teaching materials are not suited to the needs of the pupil

Schools will continually be evaluating and re-evaluating the materials they use and to a large extent the materials used will be the evidence of the philosophy which prevails within the school. The question of which materials to use is not I believe a question that can be tackled outside the department within a school, and certainly not by directive statement within a book of this sort.

What seems important to stress here is that it can be easy to take a narrow and limited view of the mathematical experiences we give pupils if the limits are dictated by just one sort of teaching material particularly if, as so often seems the case, that material limits mathematics to just number related work. Secondly the need to recognize and make provision for the use of concrete materials cannot be overstated. This latter point is seldom a difficulty in Infant and Junior schools but at the secondary stage it is all too common to see no structural or other apparatus made available.

Box 9

I recently visited a classroom where a third year secondary pupil had just received back the test completed at the end of her first set of work using the Kent Mathematics Project L material.

When asked how she had got on Catherine looked up and with a broad smile she said, 'I got ninety free per cent an' I'm really chuffed I am – you see I never got more than twenty in any mafs test I done before'.

---

6. School assessments are in conflict with a teaching model based upon meeting needs of pupils

It is important that the least able pupils *recognize* improvements made in their teaching and in their own learning as only then will they develop a more positive self-image. They are most likely to recognize improvement if they are enabled to draw a direct comparison with their previous achievements. (See Box 9.) The point of reference should be pupil's own previous performance rather than a comparison with the performance of other pupils.

To return to the reading age analogy there may be cause for great encouragement in the fact that a 10 year old pupil's reading age has advanced from 6.2 to 7.5 during the past year. The fact that this pupil is now more than 7 years of reading age below the most able, whereas at the start of the year he was only 6.2 years below does not need to be made obvious and certainly does not mean that the year's progress is worthless. Indeed we would find it exceedingly strange if we found anyone even attempting to make such an odd sort of comparison.

In mathematics, however, the use of a single test or examination right across a class or even a whole year group is frequently used to make these very comparisons between pupils in a very public way. Where this is done it can be in total conflict with the work that has been established with the pupils who have been in need of particular help with their mathematics learning and whose individual work has been sympathetically and systematically developed in response to their needs by painstaking teachers.

three

Worth and Motivation

In touching on notions like 'worth' I am all too readily aware that we could get lost in a guagmire of definitions and meanings, indulge in lengthy discussion and still end up not clear about what we are implying. What I shall put forward here then are some comments and questions of my own not attempting to suggest that this amounts to any reasoned theory but rather a hypothesis which may be worth considering in the context of pupils and their approach to mathematics learning.

When questions of the worth of mathematics are raised or implied by pupils it is easy to be found offering a rationale which appeals to utility, i.e. if you do not learn maths you will not be able to read the bus timetable, count your change out etc. The logical conclusion is that we need mathematics to survive and the causal link back to mathematics seems easy to verify. In reality, the pupil probably suspects, what to us should be obvious, that lots of people survive and will continue to survive with little or no *formal* mathematical understanding. If we argue a rationale for mathematics only on the basis of utility I believe that at some point the pupil will drive a road through our arguments.

Perhaps it would be profitable to look more carefully at why pupils pose the question. Could it be that in the mind of the pupil (Box 10) the worth of mathematics is closely related to their perception of their own success and failure? To reduce it to the simplest line of argument we may imagine the pupil thinking 'I got it right, I can do it; I enjoyed getting it

---

Box 10

Steven was 6′ 2″ and a particularly disaffected fifth year secondary pupil. He loathed maths and was probably considerably under-achieving. This was not surprising since he frequently truanted to avoid mathematics. He was, however, fairly articulate. On the day I visited his classroom he was happier to talk to me rather than do the work that had been set.

Our discussion at one stage ran like this:

Q. 'I am right in thinking that you don't really like maths much?'

Steven. 'That's right. I don't often come, so you were lucky to find me here today.'

Q. 'Do you know who does like maths in this class?'

Steven. 'Yes, Sally and Alan.'

Q. 'Why do you think they like it?'

Steven. (without any hesitation)

'Well that's easy – they get it all right, don't they – they can do it.'

---

right; it is worth doing some more things like that'. If, however, the chain changes slightly the argument becomes 'I got it wrong again; I can't do it; I don't enjoy getting things wrong; why do I need to do this anyway?'

If there is some truth in this simple logic, and I believe that if we look for it the classroom abounds with evidence to support its existence, then the question posed at the end of the chain, i.e. 'Why do I need to learn this anyway?' is not in fact a search for a convincing answer but rather a rationalization to cope with the feeling of failure and inadequacy.

I venture to suggest that if we are confronted with that form of rationalization then we are undermining our own credibility with the pupils if we provide the kind of answer that seeks to give a convincing rationale. I suspect that those who have sought to argue the case of 'enjoyment, interest and fun' as a rationale may in fact be producing a far more

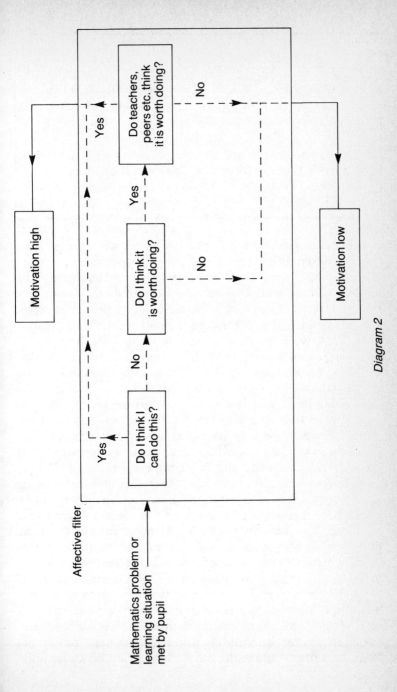

Diagram 2

Box 11

Summing up why she did not 'bother to do much maths work now' a third year secondary pupil explained a dilemma she felt she faced with her teacher:

The trouble with her is when you do try really hard and do the best you possibly can she still grumbles on at you all the time so you might just as well be grumbled at for not doing anything.

---

credible argument for youngsters who may well concede that if they could only do it they would find it enjoyable too.

Extending, then, our hypothesis and remembering the model in Diagram 1, we might expect to find considerations of the 'do I think I can do it?' variety taking precedence over and in fact probably overriding the considerations of worth. In that case we should amend our model as in Diagram 2.

Returning to worth, then, what are the implications for what we do with the pupils who have difficulties in learning mathematics?

Denscombe[14] describes in great detail the changes he has observed in the behaviour of, and strategies employed by, pupils which he sees as responses to teacher strategies for control in the classroom. It seems reasonable to argue that these sorts of intricate and changing responses could occur only if pupils were constantly observing and considering what the teacher is doing. (See Box 11.) In other words, pupils are 'reading' the attitude of the teacher to both the mathematics and to their work. A major influence on the pupils' view of 'worth' is in fact what the pupils believe to be the teacher's view of worth. So when a teacher poses the question: 'Why have you set the work out like that?' the pupil can honestly answer 'I thought that was how you wanted it to be done.' Perhaps we should spell out our priorities as teachers and classify them for the pupil. It may well be naive to believe that by withholding comments, prompts or instructions we will encourage the pupil to 'make up his own mind', for however we try to hide what we really feel the pupil will be interpreting our behaviour in some way.

In most circumstances it may not matter what view the pupil has of the teacher's priorities, likes and dislikes. However, there can certainly be circumstances where conflict arises because of a mismatch between our stated values and ideals and those we appear to support by our rewards, praise and sanctions. For example we may say we want the pupils to make estimations and so we give a lot of attention to encouraging pupils to accept that it is a legitimate activity to guess. If, however, praise and reward is given not for the 'act' of guessing but for near accurate or sensible guesses whilst we criticize or discourage inaccurate or wild guesses, the pupil will discover that the act of responding to our invitation to guess is one of high risk. Criticism or even sarcasm may be the pay off in which case the act of guessing is being inadvertently but very powerfully discouraged by the teacher.

A further point which must not be overlooked is that highlighted by Donaldson[15] who argues that the use of rewards and other extrinsic motivators may actually be counter-productive. She sees them as of little significance in comparison with the intrinsic motivators evidenced within the 'fundamental human urge to be effective, competent and independent, to understand the world and to act with skill.'

This raises the whole question of reward, praise and approval. Even if it is felt that, on balance, rewards are beneficial we must ask whether the reward systems actually reinforce the attitudes and activities we say we want to encourage? (See Box 12.) One of the unintended outcomes of using tests, of giving ticks, even of displaying pupils' work in the classroom, can easily be that of giving weight to one thing, giving it a value and worth, which places it above those things never tested, marked or displayed.

Probably within the category of things just described but worthy of particular note here is the use of apparatus. So often teachers say 'you can't go on using apparatus because the pupils think it is babyish'. Why has the view grown up that it is a more respectable thing to work with paper and pencil than it is to work with concrete materials? If the teacher of pupils who have mathematical learning difficulties

---

Box 12

In a general discussion with Mary, a second year student in the bottom band, the following arose:

Mary. 'In our set we do four sorts of maths — sometimes we do these sum books, sometimes we do our individual work in the workshop lessons, sometimes we have her (pointing at teacher) talking on the board and sometimes we have practice tests.'

Q. 'Which of these four do you think is most important?'

Mary. 'The practice tests because every half-term we have a big one like that and if you get a really good mark you go up to the next set.'

---

can do nothing else but create in them the feeling that it is legitimate to be seen working with apparatus then they have done a very great deal. A problem stems from the fact that the able pupils never use apparatus and therefore it is assumed that 'If you were good you would not need it either'. We may require a concerted effort by teachers throughout the school to give credibility to the use of apparatus in mathematics as a functional and essential means of concept formation through from early infancy to A level. How impoverished are the concepts of the A level mathematician who has never actually sat down and made solid models!

Respectability and acceptability may also be ascribed to particular mathematical activities or courses in school on the basis of where those courses lead. The influence of examinations in giving credence to courses is a factor often played upon in encouraging able pupils to perform well. A place in the examination set may be seen as a reward for good effort, hard work and attainment. Conversely the inclusion in a non-examination group can be seen as an indictment for poor performance, poor effort and so on. this criterion of worth is often reinforced by parental attitudes.

The pupil who is on a course that is not valued is therefore by implication disreputable and however much effort she or he makes will have nothing to show for it. Of even greater concern is that, when it has been implied that the reason for doing mathematics is bound up with the examination reward at the end, it becomes logical for the non-examination pupil to argue that there is now therefore no point in doing mathematics. How unenviable is the task confronting the teacher of pupils who feel justified in adopting that stance.

Both parental and peer group pressures can become critical for the pupil of low self esteem. All the encouragement given by teacher may count for very little indeed, unless approval comes also from others whose opinion the pupil values. There may be a very real need to give parents access to information about what is being planned and provided for their child. The fact that so often the pupils' insecurities and feelings of failure are intensified if parents seek to help their own children does make this a difficult area. Nevertheless, in the long term, we may give certain pupils great assistance by enlisting their parents' help in developing a positive attitude to encouraging success rather than criticizing failure. This might start by seeking the parents' help in building up a list of things the child is able to do with confidence.

Peer group pressures are perhaps the least easy to affect or control but there is little doubt that group attitudes to school are affected by comments of individual teachers. It can be thoroughly disheartening for the teacher of the least able pupils to be working in an atmosphere where the pupils in their care are the objects of humour, sarcasm and insult from their colleagues.

So far I have avoided reference to the relevance of the actual mathematics to motivation. I would assert that in most situations the question 'Is this relevant mathematics?' is far less significant than the questions of 'Can I do it?' and 'Is it worth doing?' It may even be argued that it is through these latter two questions that the pupil focuses upon the question 'Is it relevant?' If the pupils believe they are both able to do it and that it is worth doing then it becomes relevant. This lays the emphasis on factors which are intrinsic to the pupil. That there are also extrinsic factors, which confer relevance upon the mathematics work, cannot be denied. These are revealed in the context of how the mathematics is presented, and what sort of problems are posed. They will include factors like visual impact (for instance, through colour printing) couching activities in the form of games, the use of the electronic calculator, micro-computer or even just the taped lesson. Certainly these extrinsic factors will have to be considered most carefully but in practice the most impressively presented, exciting looking material is largely ineffective and often rejected by the pupil who does not believe she or he can learn from it.

Those who set a lot of store by 'making the mathematics relevant' by making it, environmental or based upon the world of work or sport are in danger of finding that their eyes are focused on quite different things to those of their pupils. It is easy to compose a list of things that we think pupils 'ought' to find interesting or 'necessary' to their lives but those teachers who have spent time listening to their pupils and talking about the world as they see it, will have found that there is an enormous margin for mismatch. If our list does happen to coincide with the pupil's view of the world then motivation may well follow from this relevance. If, however, as is all too often the case, we seem to have been thinking about a quite different world to that of the pupils we are in great danger of appearing ignorant or foolish to the pupils.

Dangerous as it is to generalize about pupils' perceptions of the world, I would suggest, on the basis of listening to pupils talking, that the significance of the world for them does not consist in objects and events in the world (i.e. places, activities, jobs, sport, spending of money etc.) but rather in the realm of feelings about themselves in the world. Moreover, these feelings seem to be so often coloured by an overriding conviction of inadequacy, failure and shame where the world becomes a hostile environment in which they will seek to cope rather than an exciting challenging field in which they will be able to demonstrate their skills and abilities. This is the context which is most 'relevant' for teacher and pupil alike.

four

The Development of Concepts

In the previous sections of this book I have concentrated more upon the pupil, the classroom, the school and the teacher than upon the mathematics. This approach has been quite deliberate, if only to demonstrate how short-sighted I believe it is to assume that all that one has to do to meet the needs of the low attainer in mathematics is to make their teachers more conversant and confident with aspects of mathematics itself. Put in another way, I believe it is totally inadequate to meet the needs of the least able pupils by paying attention only to what sort of mathematics and how to teach it. Even in turning now to the mathematics, I feel it is imperative to take a very broad view.

In recent years many reports and findings have been published which have sought to identify and analyse patterns of error. Notably these include the findings of the A.P.U.[16] and the Concepts in Secondary Mathematics and Science Project.[17] There is no doubt that such writings will stimulate very rich discussion and further work as people explore the implications of the findings.

It is tempting to take a similar analysis of errors as my starting point. However, it seems more appropriate to begin with what is revealed of the pupils' *understanding* rather than their *misunderstanding*; and to try to find what leads to understanding rather than get bogged down in a search for ways of correcting misunderstanding.

Firstly, I will consider the processes which are commonly considered to be at the heart of the development of math-

Box 13

The following excerpt comes from an essay on Concepts and Uncommon Sense in Susan Marlke, *Good Frames and Bad*, John Wiley & Sons, 1969.

The pitfalls in concept teaching are many. Perhaps the most difficult is the selection of examples. *No concept is learned from a single example*, although inspection of many texts would lead you to think that many people thought so. We can think of a concept as a class, represented, as logicians do, by a circle. In the middle of the circle, we can put the 'standard example' – the one frequently given in standard texts. If the student is given this standard example, 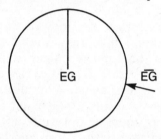 will he generalize correctly to those 'borderline' cases which an expert would include? Given a non-example, something outside the circle yet resembling members of the class in many ways, will he correctly discriminate? Anyone who has taught and tested is aware of the errors that students make along these lines, whatever the language we use to describe them. The student's concept may not go far enough – he rejects an example that experts would include in the class. Or his concept goes too far – he includes something the expert would reject. (Markle and Tiemann, 1969.)

ematics concepts and mathematical ways of thinking and then relate these to mathematically low attainers in school.

The most central activities which Skemp[18] describes are those of abstracting and classifying. It may be particularly helpful to look at the drift of Skemp's discussion in the light of a model of concept formation put forward by Markle[19] (see Box 13). Adopting Markle's model, the building up of a concept can be seen as the result of the learner making many separate discriminations related to the concept and classifying them as an example or non example. On the basis of comparisons made between examples and non examples the learner will also be abstracting rules. That this process of development is never completed is self evident in the model for not only will the learner, throughout life, add to the total discriminations made but also refine the abstraction of rules. If we are able to describe a boundary to the concept in Markle's model then clearly we could say of two discriminations close to the boundary one is an example the other is a non example. It could be argued that the boundary is likely to be more clearly defined the more the learner has had opportunity to make fine discriminations at the boundary.

In his discussion Skemp speaks of 'abstracting invariant properties' and argues that the pupil's perception of these is the machinery with which subsequent information received is classified and subsequent abstractions are made. He speaks of primary concepts which are derived from sensory and motor experiences, and secondary concepts derived from previously abstracted concepts. Hence an 'hierarchical order' of concepts is postulated where the highest order concepts are those furthest removed from the 'primary concepts'.

If we look at some of the implications of these models thus far in relation to pupils learning mathematics, the following seem worth highlighting:

> **1. There is no mathematical concept except within the mind of the person who has it; and the concept he or she has will have been built up and is being built up continuously as new perceptions and new discriminations are made**

From this it must follow that with certain pupils learning might be impaired because specific handicaps prevent certain sensory perceptions. In others, however, perceptions may not

---

Box 14

The extent to which perception varies amongst pupils is clearly demonstrated when a group are all provided with apparently the same experiences. This was brought home most forcibly to me when, for the first time, I had taken a group of third year juniors out into a street where we had agreed to look for signs of things 'that had been made by men'.

The subsequent classroom discussion led me to wonder if we had really all been in the same street, particularly when I was cast in the role of referee between arguing factions of the class over the presence or absence of things I could not recall seeing at all. Most memorable, though, was the comment of one boy who said, 'Well, all I saw was a car'.

---

be made or only partially made because of a failure to notice or to concentrate upon the information available. (Box 14) Not only must we give ample opportunity to pupils to have fundamental mathematical experiences as they see and handle concrete materials (which will increase the likelihood of making perceptions), but we must also try to establish whether or not these have been made and develop strategies for facilitating perception. The most obvious strategy here is that of promoting discussion and developing dialogue in order to focus the attention of the pupil upon what is there to be seen and experienced. In practice, however, in so many classrooms, discussion is not seen as a planned legitimate activity. It arises only if someone happens to ask or to say something.

It is important that we recognize not only perception but also the abstraction and formulating of rules as a function that must happen within the mind of the learner, if any concept is to develop. It is this function which, arguably, is the most likely to be abused in schools. The rule is given to be memorized, recalled and brought into use later rather than being abstracted by the learner. It is easy to do well, according to the criteria so often used for judging mathematics learning, provided you are an efficient rule learner and recaller. Yet it is possible to be recalling rules that simply have no real links within the pupil's concepts. The only route to recall is through memory. For the pupil who in any case has difficulties in learning mathematics this can be a recipe for disaster, confusion and defeat. In Markle's terms Egs and Eḡs must precede rules in order for the rules to have any place within a conceptual framework in the mind of the learner.

There are two important points which arise from this. Firstly it is important to consider non examples when we present our teaching points. It is only against non examples that examples can be judged yet it is not at all uncommon to find teaching material which presents only examples and assumes that pupils will generalize effectively from them. Secondly the presentation of rules first is common within many textbooks and workcards. We must be particularly careful, on this latter point, when we select materials for the least able. The worked example followed by practice is the least effective strategy for the pupil deficient in the concept. This strategy is, however, just as commonly found within teacher exposition in mathematics; and the assumption that 'if you listened more carefully you would have understood what I had meant' is one that the teacher of the least able just cannot make.

2. The presence of concrete experiences is fundamental to the development of concepts

Clearly the building blocks for the conceptual hierarchy are the lower order concepts. The richer the sensory exploration and observation of concrete materials the greater is the likelihood of appropriate discriminations being made. Hence the greater the provision for subsequent higher order concept formation. This seems almost a recurrent theme in books about learning mathematics and especially with reference to those who have difficulty learning yet in the classroom there

---

Box 15

From Skemp, *The Psychology of Learning Mathematics.*

. . . the necessary lower-order concept must be present before the next stage of abstraction is possible . . . To put this into effect, however, means that before we try to communicate a new concept, we have to find out what are its contributory concepts; and for each of these, we have to find out its contributory concepts; and so on until we reach either primary concepts or experiences which we may assume as 'given'. When this has been done, a suitable plan can then be made which will present to the learner a possible, and not an impossible task.

. . . the contributory concepts for each new stage of abstraction must be available. It is not sufficient for them to have been learnt at some time in the past. They must be accessible when needed.

---

seems to be an inordinate rush towards 'sums' and symbolic representation so that writing and recording take up the pupils' energy and thought rather concrete experiences.

3. The development of higher order concepts depends upon abstraction from lower order concepts

This statement comes almost directly from Skemp (see Box 15) and its implications must not be overlooked if real attention is to be given to the needs of the least able. The key here seems to be that the formerly developed concepts should be 'available', but with the least able pupils it is so often reported that they have great problems over recall and retention. This is the crux of so great a problem for teacher and pupil alike and the point at which so much teaching and learning can break down. A starting-point for teachers is

---

BOX 16

Recently a teacher from a special remedial unit for junior school pupils made what seemed a most perceptive comment when she said:

'It is odd really. I would never expect to ask one of my pupils to begin to do some written language work unless we had gone through quite a long process of talking and discussion first so they could talk about the words they were going to use and yet I can never remember ever discussing a piece of mathematics like that before asking them to get started.'

BOX 17

I was asked by a teacher, whose pupil had been asked to say what special things he noticed about a diagram of a square.

'What do I do about this answer?'

The pupil had said: 'Its sides are all the same and it's got square corners.'

I wonder what your reply to the teacher would have been.

---

whether this pupil has recalled sufficient of the appropriate lower order concepts for a start to be made. If not, is this because (a) learning has not yet been established in that part of the conceptual framework or (b) the pupil who previously understood, has not now retained or recalled? Far too often the teacher's activity in introducing new work is based upon the hope that neither (a) nor (b) is true. In practice, either (a) or (b) is very likely to be true with the least able pupil and probably many other pupils also. A suitable response to (a) must surely be either to conclude that the pupil is not ready yet for this work or that some specific remedial help is needed before a start is made. A suitable response to (b) would be to design some kind of revision, prompting or attention-focusing exercise in order to bring about that recall. (Box 16)

Returning to the main drift of the discussion of concept formation we must not overlook the importance of language. There are two aspects of language which it seems particularly necessary to mention here.

1. Language as a facilitator of concept development in mathematics

The further is the abstraction from sensory experiences then the more significant and precise the language with which mathematics is communicated. The learner will be developing language related to the mathematics continually. With pupils who have learning difficulties twin dangers exist: of teaching using language which is complicated or precise beyond the level of that of the learner or of failing to give ample opportunity to the learner to talk about the mathematics as she or he sees it.

It is very easy indeed to stifle the language and self-expression of the learner by appearing to anticipate the language they *should* use rather than encouraging free expression and accepting whatever language they do use. (Box 17) Perhaps too much emphasis has been laid upon what is called 'Correct mathematical language' and not enough on pupils' mathematical language.

2. Language for instruction in mathematics

Barnes[20] and others have drawn attention to the consequences upon learning of a mismatch between the sort of language presented to the learner and the sort of language the pupil uses outside school. That this and the inclusion of symbolism has an effect upon performance in mathematics has been established without a doubt (see A.P.U.). Not only the nature of the language but also a demand for written language can be a problem. In my own work with both young pupils and secondary age pupils with learning difficulties in mathematics, I have found the use of taped teaching material gives access to the mathematics in a way which written statements do not. We must not simply assume that failure to learn the mathematics in such situations is due to mathematical problems when clearly it may not be.

A further consideration arising from Skemp is what he calls 'noise'. In mathematics, he contends, most lower order concepts, from which the learner may seek to build do not have single, clear, properties but rather many properties. Some of the many properties may be relevant to the concept being built up whilst some may not. It is these irrelevent properties he refers to as 'noise' and argues that:

> In the earlier stages (of the formation of a concept) low noise with little distracting detail is desirable; but as the concept becomes more strongly established, increasing noise teaches the recipient to abstract the conceptual properties from more difficult examples . . .

For the pupil who is finding mathematical concepts hard to develop the 'noise' factor may well be absolutely critical. Much thinking effort may be wrongly applied to irrelevant distractors and even to harmful misunderstandings. It can, I suggest, also apply to concrete operations. Pupils whose workshop activity may involve cutting out circles may well have dexterity problems so that the process of cutting becomes a major hurdle and the preoccupation of all the effort and attention of the pupil. At the end of the work any mathematical significance of the planned activity may be totally obscured behind the conflicts and frustrations of the cutting activity. Might it not have been better to have supplied pre-cut circles?

A discussion of concept formation in mathematics would not be possible without some reference to Piaget.[21] Although I do not intend lengthy discussion, it is important for us to point out that if concept formation does critically depend upon the stage of 'concrete operations' becoming effectively established in the learner before readiness exists for the stage of 'formal operations' then this will be so just as much for the pupil with learning difficulties as for the pupil who learns mathematics easily. The work we plan must allow for these stages, therefore, if it is to meet the needs of the learner. However, we must be prepared to look at these stages in terms of the mathematical development rather than the age of the pupil. So often in our provision of equipment for pupils there is the tacit assumption that 'you should be past that stage by now' or that 'you should not be ready for that stage yet'. To become preoccupied with pursuing Piagetian stages may fool us into limiting the work of the pupil who is not at the same stage in all parts of her or his mathematical development. There are pupils who are quite definitely at a concrete operational stage in one part of the work but in other parts of their mathematics they are at a stage of formal operations. Our work must provide for each to develop. Further, when confronted with a situation requiring recall it may well be the case that reverting to concrete materials will provide the necessary trigger for a pupil who seems to be well past the stage of needing concrete materials. Yet another point for consideration is that completely new concepts are sometimes being met in mathematics. It would follow from the Piagetian model that each time this happens the starting point should be that of concrete operations. As I have already suggested this is just as much the case for the able student at a high level of mathematics. It is, however, seldom provided for. The able pupil may well overcome this lack but the least able pupil is very greatly disadvantaged if it is not provided for. Apparatus to support mathematics learning does not therefore have its place only at an early *age* but right through learning at an early *stage* in concept formation. Many of our least able pupils in school may well reach the age of sixteen but still be at a concrete operational stage in most of their mathematics concepts.

A further helpful view of processes involved in the development of mathematical concepts is provided by Davison and Trivett.[22] They see the processes central to the development of mathematics concepts as abstracting, relating, connecting, making models, solving problems, generalizing and specializing. They argue that these processes are normal functions of all human beings and that therefore the fundamental task of the teacher is to 'assist learners to educate themselves'. A positive effort to encourage this self education can, they suggest, be made by (a) placing responsibility for checking answers with the pupil and (b) encouraging pupils to talk about what they are doing, with the teacher keeping quiet as far as possible. Through the development of this talking about learning the vital link between apparatus, models and understanding will be made.

This emphasis on learning rather than teaching mathematics is quite definitely as appropriate with the least able and the slow learner as it is with the most able. It does, however, raise problems which must not be overlooked. Firstly, the extent to which a pupil has the facility to abstract, connect, solve problems etc. is related to the repertoire of mathematical information, skills and abstractions available to that pupil. In short the more mathematics a pupil knows the more he has to call on. When dealing with pupils who have in any case experienced great difficulty in learning mathematics the repertoire on which they can draw is likely to be small. That is not to say it should not be drawn on but if the pupil is to enjoy success in learning the teacher will have to design work with a very controlled mathematical demand and develop a very sensitive use of such material. Secondly, the extent to which a pupil has the inclination and willingness to abstract, connect, solve problems etc. must be directly related to the confidence of that pupil. The pupil who is most self confident is likely to be most ready to enter into these higher order (Box 18) activities. Conversely the pupils with the least confidence will be the least ready to enter these activities.

Emphasis on higher order activities appears to be greatly in vogue at the present time in the mathematical educational world. Teachers of the least able will have to exercise great care and considerable skill in planning to allow for these processes to have a place in the mathematics learning of their pupils. Later in this book I have given much fuller discussion to problem solving with the least able pupils.

Box 18

(Comment based upon Bloom, B. S., *Taxonomy of Educational Objectives*, Longmans, Green & Co. Ltd. (1956))

An hierarchical order of learning activities is implied in the much quoted work of Bloom, whose Taxonomy of Educational Objectives in the cognitive domain is categorized under the following headings:

KNOWLEDGE
COMPREHENSION
APPLICATION
ANALYSIS
SYNTHESIS
EVALUATION

Bloom argues that success at any of these levels depends upon previous success at the preceding levels when working in the same concept area.

There is at this point, however, a further strand which tends to be overlooked but which I believe is probably of more significance than has yet been realized. This is the whole aesthetic experience of the learner when learning mathematics. So often those who become 'hooked' on mathematics as a hobby, interest or diversion see the power of mathematics in its pattern, symmetry and order. For them equations become beautiful rather than useful, construction of solid models becomes compulsive rather than interesting and so on. In short, for some the pursuit of mathematical enquiry becomes a deeply fulfilling and engaging activity.

There is no doubt that if all our objectives in teaching mathematics to pupils are utilitarian we are in danger of missing the possibility that one reason for doing mathematics is simply that of discovering what fun mathematics can be. When dealing with the pupils who have had the least success in school we are surely dealing with pupils who experience

---

Box 19

I well remember the look of sheer pleasure and delight of a 12 year old girl who had, she claimed, for the first time in her life drawn a perfect circle.

Previously I had found her very close to tears, utterly frustrated by the odd things that kept happening to her pair of compasses. The break through had come when we abandoned the compasses and used a card strip with holes in – pin at one end and pencil at the other – to draw the circle.

---

great frustration because so often what they have produced has not looked pleasing to them. (Box 19)

I note with interest how several teachers have reported that pupils suddenly moved onto a different plane of interest and motivation when their work suddenly began to 'look nice'. So much time is spent concentrating on number related work which has little visual outcome that we reduce the chance of this 'look nice' factor occurring. There is great scope for developing diagrams and models to express number patterns and facts – whether models built with coloured cubes or even with coloured dots as an alternative to our addiction to written numbers. Much plane and solid geometry may again find justification for inclusion not because of great mathematical significance but because of the 'look nice' factor. We have a great opportunity to adorn our mathematics work area with pictures, objects from the natural world, examples of curved stitching and so on. Best of all we can draw the pupil's attention to parts of his own work where we can honestly say – 'You have made that look really good'. I would suggest that at whatever level we are teaching it behoves the teacher of mathematics to build up a repertoire of activities that are straightforward and are virtually guaranteed to produce an aesthetically pleasing outcome in order to introduce pupils to that 'look nice' factor as a means of boosting their self esteem.

five

A Closer Look at Problem Solving

It is apparent that, concomitant with a general move away from certain formal traditional mathematics involving manipulation of 'tricks', there has been a move towards open-endedness, discovery and problem-solving. Significantly the new emphasis is on process rather than product in mathematics learning.

There is a tendency, at present, to find open-ended problem-solving and investigations advocated as though these approaches should be the main vehicle for teaching mathematics to all pupils in school. It is worth devoting extra space therefore to considering problem-solving in relation to the pupil who experiences difficulty in learning mathematics.

There are considerable differences in what people mean and in what others understand by the term problem-solving. For this reason I shall take a quite detailed look at some of the literature but also it is important to consider the feedback from pupils and teachers with respect to problem-solving and the least able pupils.

The key question I would ask is this: are we able to assume that placing pupils with difficulties in learning mathematics in problem-solving situations does in fact produce the same outcomes and benefits as placing mathematically able pupils in such situations?

It is my contention, not unsupported in the literature, that we should not make this assumption. It is conceivable that the difficulties shown up in the literature arise out of which materials were used (e.g. they may depend on too high a

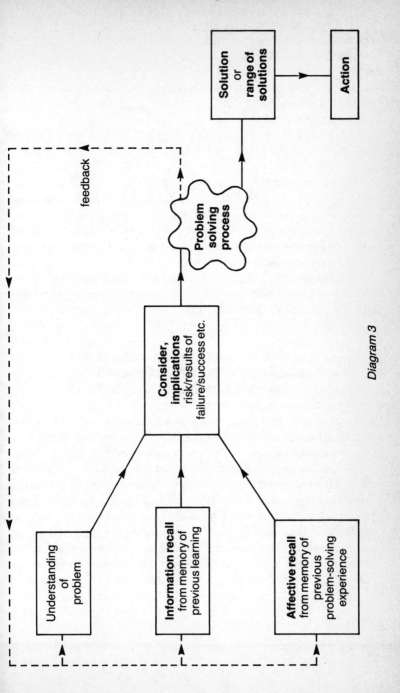

Diagram 3

reading age), or out of the particular way that the teacher organized the working within the group, or out of the school's general organization of work with the less able. However, the cause of the pupils' failure when faced with such problem-solving kind of material may actually lie within the pupil or within that learning situation.

Let us consider the model Diagram 3 as a very general description of the problem solving process in mathematics:

It is generally argued by those who advocate a problem-solving approach that it is appropriate, useful and even necessary to confront pupils with problems to solve in their learning as a preparation for the 'real world'. If we can teach them to become problem-solvers then we are equipping them with a most valuable tool for life.

At first glance, this appears to be a good rationale for a course in problem-solving but there are two questions that may require more consideration.

(a) How far can we assume that skill in problem-solving is transferable from one problem area to another?

For an adequate answer to this question our discussion would have to go far beyond the scope of this book and cannot be given the attention it deserves here. In passing, however, it is worth underlining that teachers who work with the least able often report that the lack of ability to transfer what is learned in one situation and apply it in another is one of the most commonly found and most frustrating characteristics of these pupils. Indeed, it is arguable that one of the characteristic differences between those pupils who are gifted mathematically and those who find it exceedingly difficult to learn is the facility to make connections, and to transfer their learning between one aspect of mathematics and another.

Box 20

The following is a selection of comments made by mathematics teachers using problem-solving based teaching materials with less able pupils. They are typical of many such comments made:

'They just don't seem to be able to think'.
— 3rd Year Middle School

'He will dream up a dozen other things he needs to do rather than get down to the problem'.
— 2nd Year Secondary

'Really I am the one who has to do the problems — they come to me to ask for help or reassurance on virtually every part of the work. If I don't give it, then they just produce absolute rubbish'.
— 1st Year Secondary

'They have just given up wanting to work — it has got more like a battle. They just say they don't see what the problems have got to do with them and refuse to work at them'.
— 4th Year Secondary

'Hardly any of them can read the words and those that can can't understand what they are meant to do'.
— 2nd Year Secondary

'There is a problem because all the work is different. I think they prefer being able to get into some safe routine where they know what they are expected to do'.
— 3rd Year Middle School

'I keep getting pestered to give them 'real maths'. They don't seem to mind if I give them a page of sums, but ask them to think about a problem and they just switch off'.
— 4th Year Secondary

(b) What can we take to be a suitable or true solution to a problem?

It is common to find some subjects adopt a 'coping strategy' as an alternative to a true solution when confronted with certain sorts of problem. (See Box 20) The teacher view of this is well summarized by the anguished complaint – 'I wouldn't mind so much if only they would think'. Whilst this is an understandable teacher reaction one can't help wondering if it would not be wiser to pose the questions – 'Why don't they stop to think?' or 'What do they do instead of thinking?'

If we go to many teachers in search of answers to these questions we are confronted with rationalizations and comments about pupils 'just switching off', being 'off in a world of his own' or 'doing anything rather than what I want her to', or 'Let's face it some pupils are just not ever going to be able to make any more progress at mathematics' etc.

Perhaps there is a case to be made for collecting data based on pupils' reasons for not, or 'alternatives' to, becoming involved in thinking in problem-solving situations. This would be very time-consuming but doubtless enlightening. What seems more important is to recognize that in the absence of 'thinking about the problem' some form of mental activity must be happening. If we see such happenings as alternatives to thinking, then we are wrong to say of the pupil 'he is doing nothing'.

Firstly therefore, in arriving at a hypothesis I feel it is essential to acknowledge that some form of mental activity is occurring. It seems reasonable to put into this category a whole range of strategies, frequently reported by teachers, that the less able pupil uses as means of avoiding the thinking activity planned by the teacher. Some of these are:

(a) Diversion
*– the sudden request to use the toilet, to
sharpen a pencil, return a borrowed
book etc. or irrelevant questioning or
discussion about other things, disruption
and serious misbehaviour*

This sort of behaviour is so often reported by the teacher as 'negative' behaviour. From the point of view of the pupil it might well be considered as highly effective positive behaviour directed at delaying doing what the teacher requires. Whilst, of course, such behaviour is not confined to the less able pupil, it is unquestionably a frequent occurrence with such pupils.

(b) Avoidance
*– Blank refusal to work or become
involved which even leads to walking
out or truanting*

Many teachers of the less able, particularly older pupils, speak of the problem of getting any sort of attention at all. Some have clearly settled for a truce on the basis that 'If you don't trouble me then I won't bother you'. The attitude is justified by comments like 'While there are some who do want to work I prefer to concentrate on them. I don't mind so long as the others don't interrupt me' or 'I just have to accept that there are some pupils who just don't want to work and you can't make them if they don't want to'.

At first glance this appears to be a general problem quite unrelated to problem-solving situations. On closer questioning, however, it is just these pupils about whom the teacher is so often ready to comment – 'It is all alright unless you ask them to think for themselves', or in maths particularly – 'They seem to enjoy just sitting with a page of simple adding sums and will work at it for hours, but try to do something that requires a bit of thought and they just cut right out'. The cut-out is quite definitely attributed to situations that require some sort of formulation of ideas on the part of the pupil.

(c) Heedlessness
*— Many teachers have described to me
pupils who 'just rush in'. The teachers
complain 'You might as well not bother
to try to explain what the problem is —
they leap right in and get carried away
with working on something that does
not really bear any relation to the
problem at all'*

Here the problem is not one of non-involvement but rather of wrong involvement. The pupils who do this seem to be able to embark on a wild goose chase with complete confidence and without making any alteration to their plan and ideas as a result of information gained in the process.

(d) Emotional upset
*— There are those pupils who become so
upset when confronted with problems
they cannot easily resolve that they
resort to embarrassed behaviour of one
sort or another and even, in younger
children, tears. Many teachers have
pointed out pupils who become 'so upset
that I just have to show them how to do
it'*

In complete contrast there are those whso resort to outbursts of angry behaviour or tear up their work, break apparatus and in other ways display fits of temper.

Again, this cannot be seen as behaviour confined to problem-solving situations but there seems little doubt that, for pupils who are inclined to behave in this way when faced with difficulties, problem-solving activities can easily precipitate such outbursts.

It seems reasonable therefore to suggest that the less able pupils' reluctance to become involved in problem-solving situations in school could be interpreted as opting for an alternative strategy to the problem-solving envisaged. If this is a reasonable description of the behaviour one would expect that before any meaningful problem-solving can occur with a pupil who tends to employ such a strategy, the teacher has first to enable the pupil to overcome that tendency. This appears to be implied by Lovatt[23] who, in describing his experimental work using the Nuffield approach to maths with E.S.N. pupils, points out that:

> The discovery aspect of the work needs to be carefully guided. The children do not seem to benefit from apparatus, charts or equipment in a classroom unless guided to them.

Surely the teacher guidance here consists in moving the pupils onto a problem-solving track which they do not tend to adopt without deliberate and careful guidance on the part of the teacher.

A further feature of teachers' comments is their consistent reporting of the 'constant questioning for reassurance'. Over and over again teachers report that the less able pupils tend to ask the most basic questions about every decision. Even when they can read instructions they will ask if that is what it really says. When they have listened to instructions they still come up and ask if the teacher really meant what they said.

Teachers' comments therefore seem to indicate two behavioural aspects which are common with less able pupils in most work but which come particularly into focus when pupils are confronted with decision-making in problem-solving. These are: 1. The tendency to develop alternative strategies and 2. The constant seeking for reassurance.

Turning to the literature in the fields of problem-solving, educational psychology and teaching and learning theory, I have sought to extract points related to less able pupils and problem-solving. For this reason I have paid more attention to descriptions of the conditions required for problem-solving to take place than to theoretical models of the problem-solving process in action.

I am impressed by the comparability of the observations made in the classroom, described earlier and the findings of Kagan.[24] As a result of his empirical work on pupils in problem-solving situations involving uncertainty and there-

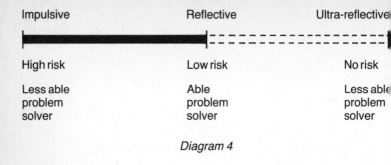

Impulsive	Reflective	Ultra-reflective
High risk	Low risk	No risk
Less able problem solver	Able problem solver	Less able problem solver

Diagram 4

fore requiring decisions to be made, he describes a dimension with impulsive behaviour and reflective behaviour at its poles.

From my own observations of junior and secondary low attaining pupils in problem-solving situations I would suggest that less able subjects are represented in both the impulsive and reflective categories. However, I would argue further that there is a qualitative difference in the reflective behaviour of the successful problem-solver and the reflective behaviour (which I shall call ultra-reflective behaviour) of some less able or low attaining pupils.

It may well be that in the case of this ultra-reflective behaviour the drive towards avoiding failure is so great that the pupil becomes totally defensive and develops mechanisms by which she or he cuts out completely from the problem-solving situation. This would certainly match the descriptions of teachers who so consistently use such terms as 'withdrawn', 'in a world of his own', 'on a different wavelength altogether' to describe such pupils. It would then extend Kagan's two groups and therefore extend the dimensions which might be broadly related to success in problem-solving and acceptance of risk as in Diagram 4.

Describing the 'dynamics of failure', Combs and Snygg[25] place the major emphasis on the part played by feelings of inadequacy which they argue arise from a failure to meet deep psychological needs. (Box 21)

If this sort of view of inadequacy and self-image can arise in every aspect of living, it does not seem incongruous to argue that the perceptions of the self which relate specifically

---

Box 21

From Combs and Sugg, *Individual Behaviour, a Perceptual Approach to Behaviour.*

From birth to death man is continually engaged in the search for greater feelings of adequacy. Whether or not he is successful in this quest will be determined by the perceptions he is able to make in the course of his lifetime . . .

. . . whereas adequate persons see themselves as capable of coping with life, inadequate people have grave doubts about their capacities to deal with events. Their experience has taught them that they are more often than not unliked, unwanted, unacceptable or unworthy. Seeing themselves in these ways, inadequate personalities find living a difficult and hazardous process . . .

. . . such people find no rest or contentment for life is a continual contest in which they daily run the risk of destruction. If the self is defined in too negative a fashion, the individual may even give up in despair. He may accept himself as defeated and incapable of dealing with life.

---

to school will come sharply into focus during the pupil's school career. Feelings of specifically educational inadequacy would therefore become a force with far-reaching effects upon the learner. Combs and Snygg put forward the suggestion that an adequacy–inadequacy continuum can be described onto which all people could be plotted as in Diagram 5.

Application of this sort of continuum to an educational setting would also seem to fit in with the views of theorists like Stones[26] (See Box 22).

In relation to problem-solving approaches then the question that would inevitably have to be asked is whether there might be different responses to the same problem situations by subjects who are at different points on such a continuum.

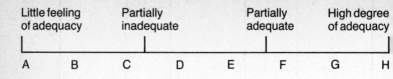

Little feeling of adequacy		Partially inadequate			Partially adequate		High degree of adequacy
A	B	C	D	E	F	G	H

Diagram 5
Note. This is a copy of Fig. 22 from Combs and Snugg,
Individual Behaviour, revised edition, p.266

BOX 22

From Stones, E., *An Introduction to Educational Psychology*.

The fact that backward children are often suffering from emotional problems presents difficulties in treating them . . .
. . . Negative affect will act as a powerful inhibitor of learning . . . Having probably had little if any encouragement before school and having been subjected to more than usual inconsistency in the schedules of reinforcement by parents, such children will lack confidence, will shrink from the unknown, whether it be a new situation or problems in learning. Lacking experience of consistent reinforcement, they will tend to abstain from any new activity which, so far as they know, will be punished.

Feelings of adequacy or inadequacy are likely to have maximum effect in situations involving uncertainty and the requirement to make decisions. In short, decisions involving risk. In their study of cognition and personality, Kogan and Wallach[27] sought to investigate the effects of a whole range of personality traits upon risk-taking and problem-solving. Their findings suggest that in many cases the characteristics under test have such profound effects upon the subject's approach to problem-solving that it becomes impossible to accept any single model of problem-solving as likely to be universally applicable to pupils. In discussing the commonly argued controversy between problem-solving as a unitary process as distinct from a multi-process view, they point out:

> It is the particular motivational matrix within which thinking activities occur that determines its dimensionality. Where test anxiety and defensiveness are high, risk-conservatism considerations seem to be highly salient, with the consequence that most of the thinking tasks used are approached from that perspective.

There is little doubt that test anxiety and defensiveness, as they use the terms, are likely to be present in less able pupils.

Moving on further from the mere fact of the presence of possible causes of differences in approach to problem-solving, there is, in the literature, considerable reference to the outcomes of such differences.

Klausmeier and Loughlin[28] studied the characteristics of children of different levels of intelligence, as measured by I.Q. tests, in solving problems. Even when teaching problems were apparently suited to the particular ability of the pupils they found that the low ability groups showed less persistence, greater acceptance of incorrect solutions and greater use of random attack. Conversely the high ability groups took greater note of mistakes and their correction, verification of solutions and logical sequence in problem-solving.

De Cecco[29] suggests that experimental findings indicate the presence of 'set' and 'direction' in problem-solving. Pupils respond to problems when they recognize the 'set' or 'direction' they think appropriate to the problem. But he points out:

> Whether solution attempts will be successful or not will depend upon the relevance of the response system to the requirements of the particular problem.

Describing Duncker's work, Peel[30] comments:

> When a person finds a problem impossible he tends to alter its content conditions ... weakness in capacity to generalize efficiently was found to be a significant factor in poorer performers.

Other writers also indicate the presence of factors within the pupils which may well lead to variation in the effectiveness of learning through problem-solving for a particular pupil:

Garry and Kingsley[31] state that:

> Performance (in problem-solving) is affected by the expectations for success and this in turn depends upon the degree of success or failure experienced.

Bruner[32], in arguing the importance of problem-solvers reaching a stage when they can assess the higher order relevance of their own efforts, points out:

> The ability of the problem-solvers to use information correctively is known to vary as a function of their internal state. One state in which information is least useful is that of strong drive and anxiety . . . Another such state has been referred to as functional fixedness.

In commenting on Maltzman's theory of problem-solving, De Cecco suggests that failure to solve problems can be attributed to 'generalized inhibition from repeated unsuccessful occurrences of the dominant incorrect response' and also to 'high irrelevant drive such as anxiety'.

Returning then, to my first 'key question' about problem-solving, I shall pose a similar second question: How far can we assume that the less able pupil is likely to approach problem-solving in the same way as the more able pupil and what might be the nature of the differences in their approach?

Bogoiavlenski and Menchinskaia[33] describe the characteristics of the lowest level of problem-solving (See Box 23). Their observations match closely those of Duncker.[34]

These writings and in fact the classroom observations on which they are based do not refer to any tendency by the pupils to develop alternative strategies.

Most writers simply do not treat the question which is in front of pupils of *whether to become involved with or whether to avoid problem-solving*.

This is noticeable in the writing of Lindsey and Norman[35] where they write:

BOX 23

From Bogoiavlenski and Menchinskaia in Simon and Simon *Educational Psychology in the U.S.S.R.,* (1963).

The lower level is characterised by the following: general lines for the solution of the problem are entirely absent, the conditions of the problem are broken down into familiar partial tasks so that each is solved in an habitual way without cognition of the conditions as a whole; there is a fixation on some of the most frequently used ways of thought. There takes place, therefore, an actualisation of well reinforced methods of solution, i.e. synthesis is used without adequate analysis of the conditions of the problem.

This phenomenon finds clearer expression in cases of pathological disturbance of cerebral activity. In this case methods of action are not determined by the conditions of the problem (as a whole) but, on the contrary, habitual methods of action lead to a reconstruction of the conditions of the problem. This fact is also noted by I. M. Soloviev in study of intellectually backward children. He notes that if the child does not find himself in a position to change and adapt his knowledge to the conditions of the task set, he 'changes the conditions of the task, adapting them to his potentialities'. M. I. Kuzmitskaia has also studied pupils of special schools and noted that a similar transformation of the conditions of problems often takes place along the lines of reproduction of the conditions of formerly solved problems'.

A Person recalling material seems to be solving a problem. First he analyses the question to decide whether it is legitimate, whether he is likely to have the information and if so, how difficult it will be to find. If he decides to attempt a recall, he sets up a retrieval strategy . . .

1	2	3	4
Thinking and learning styles	Mathematical concepts/skills/ methods	Enquiry skills and procedures	Attributes of the problem-solver

Diagram 6

they then go on to describe subsequent stages in arriving at the solution. The very fact that they use the statements *'decide whether it is'*, *'whether he is likely to have'*, *'if so'* and *'if he decides'* suggests a reasonable possibility for the answer to be negative in each case. Surely if one might ask what would be the outcome of a negative answer, then the whole issue must be problematic.

Burton[36] suggested four areas of importance in problem-solving, which she uses as column headings in a table as shown in Diagram 6.

Having spoken of the difficulties of knowing the teaching/learning background of each pupil, she argues that:

> The teacher needs also to accept the combination of abilities that create good problem-solvers are probably equally inaccessible. Given two students of roughly equal developmental level, they will cope quite differently with a problem; indeed, the same student will be successful on one occasion, unsuccessful on another, as one knows with one's own problem-solving. It is therefore suggested that it would be helpful for teachers to limit their own areas of responsibility, so that the range of objectives and consequent activities is within the bounds of possibility. It is simply not feasible to ask every teacher, primary and secondary, to be a diagnostic psychologist, a social-psychologist, a sociologist, sometimes with anthropological implications, and an educator with the appropriate knowledge, skills and techniques.

With reference to her column headings, she says:

> Columns 1 and 4 display the learner's input and output. These are, in the main, inaccessible to teaching and consequently empty from the point of view of a teacher's planning.

Box 24

The following excerpt comes from Rohwer, Ammon and Cramer *Understanding Intellectual Development*, 1974.

An example from the classroom:

First, as the tension associated with the need to solve the problem increases, the discomfort may become too great. The child may be unable to contain the mounting psychological pressure, and all at once this tension is released in an outburst of *affect*. The frustrated young student, unable to solve his math problem, instead begins to kick the desk, the wall, or other students, to run around the room, to yell or sing or be otherwise 'disruptive'. These behaviors help reduce his level of internal discomfort, but of course they do nothing to gratify the need for mastery and competence. In the end, the original need is no closer to being fulfilled than it was at the beginning of this sequence. For this reason, because the need remains ungratified, and drive tension has been only partly reduced, we can expect this sequence of events to be continually repeated. The child's acting up is no more than a temporary relief; his real need -- to be able to solve the problem given him -- has not been met. When the child is able to attain that goal, the acting-up behaviour will disappear . . .

A second outcome of this situation -- in which the child is given a problem to solve for which the answer is not immediately forthcoming -- is that the child will lapse into a state of daydreaming and fantasy, that is, into primary process thinking. Unable to solve the problem in reality, the child may fall into a daydream in which he has not only figured out this problem, but in fact is such a mathematical whiz that he is about to plan the first space module to fly to Venus. The elaboration of this fantasy into the child's imagining himself to be so competent in mathematics that all the great scientists in the world must come to consult him provides some degree of drive gratification, in that it clearly fulfills the need for competence and mastery – at least on the fantasy level. But the fantasy stands in marked contrast to the reality of the situation – that he cannot figure out his fourth-grade math problem. The original need remains unfulfilled. While the psychological tension will continue to increase. Both the child who acts up and the child who is daydreaming (or not paying attention, or is uninterested, or however else this retreat into fantasy is labeled) remain in a condition of psychological tension and discomfort. Although their behavior provides them with some temporary and partial gratification, they do not experience any basic satisfaction . . . Unfortunately, their methods for discharging painful inner tension bring them no closer to a feeling of fulfillment and pleasure.

The third possible outcome of this situation requires the use of mental mechanisms to temporary restrain and delay the immediate discharge of accumulating psychological energy and instead to channel this energy into activating those cognitive processes that will be of use in arriving at the solution of the problem. By searching through the memory store, by the use of secondary thought processes, by trying out different approaches both in thought and action, the child may eventually reach for the solution to the problem. The need for mastery and competence is then fulfilled through his own efforts and activity, and he experiences a feeling of satisfaction and pleasure. Although the satisfaction was not so immediate as with the other two examples, the basic need has been met, and in that sense the satisfaction is more genuine.

It seems to beg many questions if one is to argue that because things are inaccessible they are not problematic. If they are accepted as problematic surely they must receive consideration in designing a course.

The literature is full of references to the work of Gagné.[37] It is interesting to note that he makes reference to the importance of recognizing the 'internal variables' i.e.

the activity of problem-solving is a natural extension of rule learning, in which the most important part of the process takes place *within the learner*. The solving of a problem may be guided by a greater or lesser amount of verbal communication supplied from the outside, but the most essential variables are internal ones. It is particularly significant to note that the components which appear to make problem-solving possible are the rules that have previously been learned. Problem-solving may be viewed as a process by which the learner discovers a combination of previously learned rules that he can apply to achieve a solution for a novel problem situation.

But he takes as given that the process actually takes place or *will* take place within the learner provided the previous rules were learned, regardless of the psychological make-up of the learner.

Non-involvement on grounds other than that the rules were not previously learned does not appear to be even conceived of. Again Gagné does not make allowance for the fact that 'becoming involved in problem-solving' could be problematic, but since he is more particularly concerned about what happens, once the subject starts to become involved, this is perhaps not surprising.

Rohwer, Ammon and Cramer[38] do, however, start from the premise that becoming involved *is* problematic. They suggest the model shown in Diagram 7.

When we consider the less able pupil in the problem-solving situation it is this aspect of alternative strategies which comes so clearly into focus.

Burner[39] makes detailed reference to observations and conclusions which also support the view of alternative activities to 'effective learning' of which he sees problem-solving as a vital part. His observations were made amongst pupils who were specifically referred to guidance clinics because of 'learning blocks'.

Preliminary observation of such children has led us too simply to the conclusion that it was not so much that they had grave difficulties in learning as that they seemingly learned in such a way that there was little or no transfer to new situations, in consequence of which they were constantly having to learn *de*

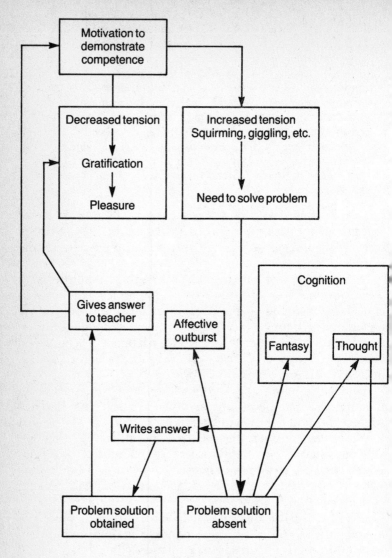

Diagram 7 Reactions of fourth grade children to difficult mathematics problems

Note: This model and the description of the classroom observations it seeks to illustrate (see Box 24) certainly allows for the development of alternatives to becoming involved in problem-solving in the classroom. Indeed, their description is clearly congruent with those situations which have given rise to the comments of teachers described in Box 20.

novo. There is a little truth to this observation, but it is quite trivial. . . .

It became apparent after some months of work that the learning activities of our disturbed children had certain distinctive features. . . .

In a word, their efforts to defend themselves from the activity of learning and from its consequences made it extremely difficult for them to get to the activity of 'school learning' itself. Their schoolwork created certain psychological problems that were much more compelling than school problems and that drastically altered their approach to conventional school learning. They could not, in short, cope with the demands of schoolwork unless and until they were able to defend themselves against the panic of impulse and anxiety that the demands of schoolwork set off in them. . . .

It was not that they were unable to learn in the conventional sense of the word – for in fact there was much learned canniness in their defensiveness against learning, and later there was often much talent in the way in which they approached school problems when the clamor of defense requirements had been in part quieted. . . .

The affective links that relate concepts and ideas often are powerful and relatively intractable, in the sense that they persist in fantasy and can be found to intrude in the child's thinking in later school settings.

This view is also supported by the experimental study carried out by Schroder and Hunt.[40] In seeking to open up the whole question of the relationship between personality factors and problem-solving behaviour, they focused on conditions involving failure and criticism. On the basis of their reactions to failure in problem-solving situations they classified subjects' behaviour into avoidant and non-avoidant categories. On failing, the non-avoidant subject 'persisted in looking for other solutions with a minimum of disruption in performance' whilst the avoidant subject 'defended himself against failure by behaving in such a way as to prevent the occurrence of any situation which he might have to interpret as failure'. They comment:

Individuals may avoid making negative interpretations (of their own adequacy) by a host of defensive interpretations, e.g., they may think 'this is too difficult for anyone to do . . .

I'm alright however', or 'I was just unlucky'. Indeed, the entire gamut of defences emanating from avoidance processes may be considered as functioning to prevent interpretations of 'personal inadequacy'.

Again, Bruner argues that experimental evidence of an unexpectedly high self-evaluation of some retarded readers reflects a coping process. An unrealistically high self-evaluation is maintained as a means of denying and coping with failure. Certainly this argument finds support in the work of Nichols, S.L., Nichols, K.A. and Burden[41] who made a close study of the apparent paradox between low competence in reading coupled with high self-evaluation. If these arguments have substance and should thus be equally applicable to problem-solving, then they would seem to provide a basis for explanation for the impulsiveness of the less able pupils to which I referred earlier.

On the basis of all this discussion therefore I suggest that it is both more realistic and more helpful if what we really have in mind is a modification of the model shown in Diagram 3 which amended is shown in Diagram 8.

Significantly I have added the possible route through coping or avoiding strategies to alternative forms of behaviour. On the basis of this I would argue that if we are to introduce the least able or unsuccessful pupils to problem-solving in mathematics we have got to pay a great deal of attention to minimizing the pupils' perception of risk, in an endeavour to increase the self confidence of the pupil.

Making decisions and acting upon them involves risks. Perhaps all too often the problems with which we confront pupils are requiring them to make a very wide range of decisions – in their eyes far too wide to be worth taking the risk and so they opt out. We are faced with a difficult judgement about 'removing' decisions for we fear that 'spoon feeding' will lead to pupils not becoming self-reliant. On the other hand if we do not remove some of the decisions we may well cause the pupils to be defeated before they start. Surely if we are to make an error in judgement at this point is is far wiser to err on the side of providing too much help initially rather than too little. For the pupil who is finding risks

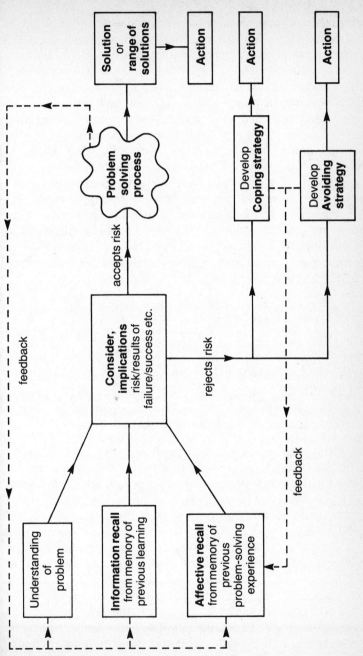

Diagram 8   Augmented version of problem-solving model

minimal it is easy to increase the decisions to be made as confidence grows but for the pupil who is finding risks too great we are creating the very climate of failure which we hope to avoid.

Those teachers who, in the past, have operated at the 'never provide the pupils with an answer' end of the spectrum have clearly intended to provide the maximum opportunity for the pupil to be reinforced by success but for the least able such an approach can be totally destructive. The degree to which problems presented are open-ended and require decisions to be made must be seen in relation to the confidence, at the time, of the learner who confronts the problem.

There appear to have been conflicting ideas in the literature about the part played by language in problem-solving, but great emphasis is placed on it by Gagné and Smith[42] who summarized their findings in a study of the effects of verbalization on problem-solving thus:

> requiring subjects to verbalise during practice has the effect of making them think of new reasons for their moves and thus facilitates both the discovery of general principles and their employment in solving successive problems.

Also, Samson[43] makes it clear that:

> thinking is largely a matter of using words in various different meanings. . . . We become increasingly aware of things as we develop increasingly discriminating vocabularies.

For the purposes of planning problem-solving work for the least able it would seem right to have as an ultimate goal a stress on using language in presenting solutions. This is in itself not likely to be an easy task since classroom observations make it abundantly clear that those who have difficulties in learning mathematics are the very pupils who seem to have the greatest problem in using language to describe their thought processes. Whilst it would seem right to agree that we should aim at the pupils developing 'increasingly discriminating language', there is usually a great deal to be achieved before the pupil can be confident in this respect.

I am attracted by the stages in the development of problem-solving outlined by Peel[44] where he links a developmental

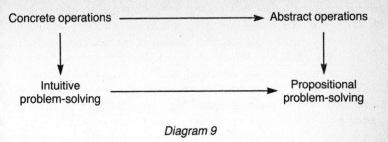

Diagram 9

view of problem-solving with the Piagetian view of concept development. The sort of relationship shown in Diagram 9 is implied.

This would seem to suggest that it is wise to seek to give pupils ample opportunity for success in intuitive problem-solving, in which language may play a very small part, before moving towards propositional problem-solving where the place of language is likely to be more central.

As suggested earlier, so often that stage which is most neglected in the development of mathematics with pupils in school is that stage where encouragement and opportunity can be given for the pupil to put in his or her own words, without fear or threat of correction, statements which summarize how they see the mathematical situation. Time must be given and work must be planned so that there is an obvious point at which the pupil has opportunity to make a personal and original response. This in itself will require great confidence on the part of the learner.

Recognizing and receiving a problem as a real problem may also be something that varies from pupil to pupil or certainly from user to user. Unless the problem is seen as a problem by the pupil there is always going to be that feeling of play acting and artificial interest — if not rejection on the grounds of irrelevance. In a fascinating discussion about an approach made through fiction and fantasy Dyson[45] argues the case for a definition of 'real problems' in terms of a pupil 'finding a solution which seems important for its own sake'. Context may therefore need just as much thought and attention by the teacher as content.

Great care must be taken over formation of working groups for the problem-solving activities. In principle, it seems essential to regard the problem-solving needs of each pupil as utterly individual. For this reason it seems wise to seek to design individualized tasks which make specific allowance for the pupil's own strengths, weaknesses and interests and thereby provide the greatest opportunity for success.

There must be allowance for exceptions to this general principle so that we may reap any benefits which might come from having paired or group working. For instance, we may wish to pair or group:

(a) Where we have pupils who do appear to be at such a similar stage that cooperative working is likely to lead to an equal contribution and benefit for each pupil.
(b) Where the opportunity to speak to someone else is provided in order to encourage verbalizing with the purpose of clarifying the thoughts and concepts of the speaker.
(c) Where it is deliberately planned to provide a range of viewpoints or ideas out of which the solution should arise. It must be noted that this form of sharing is only likely to produce real open discussion if the teacher or some other skilful 'chairman' is involved.
(d) Where for particular reasons it is felt desirable to expose a pupil to social contact to aid personality development which is judged to be more important at that particular stage than the development of problem-solving.

Exception (d) is particularly important since amongst the less able in schools there is a high proportion of pupils with particular personality problems. To advocate individualized working for some whose real need is to become integrated with others in school might well be unwise. Conversely, to insist on social integration may be unwise for those who are unable to cope with social contact at this stage. Integration in groups would also seem to be pointless for those pupils who become adept at operating coping strategies which specifically arise from the group situation, e.g. copying, relying on

Box 25

I recently watched a situation created by a teacher in which a class of secondary low ability girls were being given 'problems' to solve. One pair had a problem presented in which they had an uncalibrated jug of water known to hold 7 litres but they had to put exactly 6 litres in another uncalibrated jar.

In order to solve the problem they were supplied with a variety of different sized vessels including a calibrated measuring cylinder.

The pupils considered the problem, looking rather mystified but touching none of the vessels. No action had taken place when after a few minutes the teacher came to see 'how they were progressing'.

'Have you any ideas?' she asked. The serious reply came from one: 'We could drink the first litre.' This was received as a piece of good fun and pleasant laughter on the part of the teacher was taken up by the two girls. Teacher then went over the problem again explaining the nature of all the vessels. For the whole period of working neither girl touched or looked at in detail any of the vessels. Both looked vexed and proffered no solution. A series of visits to 'see' by teacher revealed no offer of a solution from the pupils. There was rising embarrassment and confusion on the part of the pupils and increasing frustration on the part of the teacher. In the end teacher proceeded to make very direct leading questions to which the inevitable answers sometimes came from the pupils but were usually supplied by the teacher.

It would not be easy to summarize what was learned by the pupils in doing this 'problem' but it would certainly have included that – if you say what you really think and it is not right you will be laughed at!

others to make decisions, agreement with majority view without real consideration of ideas, etc.

If we intend to replace the syndrome of reinforced failure and its consequent expectation of failure with an expectancy for success then it is essential that pupils know when they have been successful. However, if emphasis is on the process of problem-solving it becomes more difficult to encourage success. It is the 'seeking to find a solution' that must be seen by the pupil to be successful rather than recognition of the particular solution arrived at. The course must not encourage the pupil in the view that 'getting the right answer' is what is valued above all else. If we genuinely aim to promote confidence in 'seeking' solutions, where the emphasis is on the seeking, we must develop ways of encouraging the search activity as being evidence of success even if the solution offered is unsuccessful or incorrect. Great care must be taken that we do not intervene in the pupils' search procedure in order to lead them more directly to the solution we want them to find. (Box 25) The comments from the teacher of the 'try doing it like this' variety may utterly destroy the confidence we are seeking to build up. The whole 'teacher's way must be best' attitude has to be broken down, both in the teacher and the pupil. Beard[46] points out:

> Teachers who solve all the problems, displaying their own superior skills, tend to depress interest in all but their most able pupils.

six

From Why to How

The notion of identifying examples of 'good practice', studying such practice in action and then disseminating information about it has been very central to curriculum development in the last few years. Occasional observers, who seek to look in depth at the classrooms where 'good practice' had been identified or recommended, have necessarily looked beyond the practices to the rationale which gives rise to them. It is quite possible that excellent practice can exist in classes where it is apparently quite unsupported by a deliberately considered rationale. In such situations, teachers will justify their work by saying 'Well, it just seemed to suit my pupils best if I did it that way'. Such intuitive development has often led to some of the most appropriate curriculum changes within a school.

I would suggest that in situations like this, teachers have responded to the unvoiced but pressing question of 'What shall I do with these pupils?'. By seeking to answer it practically, they have confronted the question 'How shall I do it with these pupils?'.

Others have approached the whole matter of teaching mathematics from a theoretical basis, by first posing such questions as 'What is the nature of mathematics?' and 'Why should we teach it?'. Having developed and considered a rationale, they then must also move towards the question 'What shall we teach?'. This chain of theoretical considerations can have no impact on the pupils until the same practical question is tackled, i.e. 'How shall we do it with these pupils?'. Either way, the vital question which cannot be avoided is related to 'How should we teach this?'. We can easily seem justified, therefore, when the major part of our in-service education in mathematics is taken up by providing for teachers' answers to the question 'How should we do this?'.

It must be clear, however, from the previous chapters that I have attached greater importance to developing an appropriate rationale for teaching mathematics to the low attainer than to providing model practices and techniques for teachers. The reason I do this is because I have seen a lot of work break down in schools where particular teaching approaches, use of materials or schemes of work have been implemented but without recognition or adoption of the philosophy behind them. In contrast, where teachers have first taken on board the philosophy and rationale behind such work, there is then a quite different attitude and approach.

It would, however, be totally inappropriate to try to pass on to teachers a philosophy and rationale without also attending to the question 'How shall we teach this?'. 'When?', teachers would ask, 'are we getting down to the nitty gritty of the classroom?'. At this point, therefore, I shall seek to describe a pattern of individualized learning which I believe can very suitably embrace the rationale developed in earlier chapters and which is also becoming a pattern for good practice in many classrooms.

The system described is basically that developed by Bertram Banks at Ridgewaye School, Southborough, and was based on his own childhood experience in the 1920s in West Ham of the Dalton Plan.

Mr. Banks' refined system then became the central feature of both the Kent Mathematics Project, which he directed, and the Secondary Mathematics Individualized Learning Experiment (SMILE), which was developed in ILEA after the model was tried out in ILEA schools in 1969. The basic tenets of the system are as follows.

Each pupil will have planned for her or him a set of assignments to be done over the next few workshop sessions. The variety and nature of the assignments will be decided upon by the teacher, who in planning them will consider both the pupil's previous mathematics experience and performance, and also other factors related to the pupil's special needs. During the workshop sessions, therefore, all pupils have separate work pre-planned for them which they will do assignment by assignment working at their own rate, not at a rate geared to the whole group.

Provided the assignments are drawn from appropriate sources and are pitched at an appropriate level, pupils are likely to be readily involved from the start. This is based on the assumption that the pupils have been assigned tasks that are clear and manageable and that there need not be constant demands on teacher for help. Ideally, the assignments will be designed so that they can be marked by pupils themselves.

In a well ordered and well organized workshop of this sort, the pupils will also accept responsibility for collecting and replacing apparatus and materials, leaving the teacher free to concentrate on help over the mathematics. Often this will amount to responding to individual questions from pupils, often it will mean teacher promoting a discussion or raising a question with an individual pupil. Sometimes it will involve the teacher planning to work with a small group within the class for a part of the lesson. The opportunity also exists to set up groups working at a task in common from their assignment, so creating a means of discussion and sharing of ideas. It is against the background of high involvement of pupils in their own work that the teacher is able to create the time to listen and talk to individual pupils about mathematics.

I shall digress from the description of the model at this point to voice the concern so often raised – 'But where does the teaching come in?'. Without any intention of playing with words, surely the much more significant question should be 'Where does the learning come in?'. Those who are advocating forms of individualized learning place their trust in the interaction between the learner and the learning materials – active involvement being the key. Therefore, the nature of assignments given to facilitate such learning must be very carefully selected. The teacher or other pupils may be alongside to discuss, raise questions and make comments, but it is as the assignment progresses that the learning takes place. This is, of course, in considerable contrast to the conventional situation where first the teacher presents the teaching points and looks for the learning to take place in the learner. Having done this, work at that level is then assigned to the pupil.

Many teachers have found it hard to accept that the pupils can be placed in a learning situation without having prior teaching presented and have been surprised to discover how mature pupils, even of very low ability, have been in accepting a greater responsibility for their own learning.

The key role of the teacher has shifted from being an expositor of mathematics to a director and tutor of individual pupils. The emphasis has swung from presenting mathematics teaching to promoting mathematics learning.

When such a system is well organized and is supported both by careful monitoring of pupils' on-going work and by testing to reveal significant problems with work at the completion of the set of assignments, it can be a particularly efficient way of working.

In order to get the very best out of such a system of working, the teacher will want to:

1. Create constant opportunities to talk to the pupils about their work.
2. Provide a wide variety of topics and approaches to the work.
3. Give full opportunity to introduce investigations and free choice activities in which the knowledge and skills developed can be given application.
4. Ensure that the progression or pacing through the work is such that every pupil experiences a high level of success in what she or he does and is continually encouraged to be working at a rate which is challenging.
5. Provide regular and frequent feedback to the pupil over test results.
6. Give additional time to other mathematics work, including class discussion, and repeated practice work.
7. Keep a continuous record of work completed.
8. Monitor carefully the proper use of the self marking procedure.

There is no reason why this basic method of working may not embrace a wide range of teacher-made and published material. However, care must be taken to ensure that, as far as possible, the material is effectively self-instructional, otherwise the burden of questions falling upon the teacher will be so great as to make the whole operation unmanageable. The inclusion of some self-instructional computer programs, tape material, mathematical games and problems is ideal.

In a well-organized workshop atmosphere with suitably selected assignment work effectively planned to match pupil needs, the teacher will be enabled to have time available to spend with individual pupils dealing with mathematics. Many teachers working in this way, whilst agreeing it is very demanding on them, are finding themselves becoming much more aware of the individual problems, strengths and weaknesses, etc., of the pupils. Both they and the pupils are becoming used to private discussion, which they find far less threatening and inhibiting than public discussion of learning problems. The same sorts of opportunity and benefit arise, as have been noted by Graves[47], in developing his technique of conferencing for the development of language and writing skills. It would be quite wrong to pretend that this level of contact is commonplace or easy to set up in the classroom where individualized teaching in mathematics is in practice, but there is no doubt that it is of the utmost benefit bo both teacher and learner where it is done.

Arguably, the greatest benefit in working in this way derives from the fact that the pupils do work at such very different rates and have clearly different levels of mathematical performance, yet each can be having a highly successful performance within the work assigned. This will mean that, very suitably, pupils will be at different levels of attainment within the group after a short time, even if they all had the same starting point. This in itself raises the greatest problem about such a pattern of working, since it tends to conflict with the way in which pupils are conventionally assessed.

Hitherto the giving of a test in common to all the pupils enables the teacher to generate the information – 'Given this test, pupil A got x%', 'Given the same test, pupil B got y%'. However, given the pattern that develops from the individualized work described, it becomes more appropriate to say:

'Pupil A is capable of a mark of x% at this level of test'
'Pupil B is capable of a mark of x% at this level of test'.

Implied in this, therefore, is the need for a set of tests across a range of levels, a model which indeed fits in with much educational thinking at the present time.

The several points at which assessment will be important within a system of this sort can be summarized under three headings.

Initial assessment

Since it is not intended that the programme of work to be planned for each pupil is pre-determined by the age of the pupil, syllabus for the year group or any other factor outside the pupil, it is necessary to discover what are the needs of the pupil in relation to mathematics. With the low attainer, such an assessment will need to be based upon a mixture of informal discussion, observing the pupil when given a task to do and written answers to oral or written questions. The intention will be to try as far as is possible to reveal those aspects of the pupil's understanding of mathematics which have developed and those which have not. On the basis of this evidence, the teacher will plan the first set of assignments for the pupil. It will have been the intention of the teacher to start at a point which capitalizes on what the pupil is able to do, moving gradually on into less familiar ground.

Monitoring of progress

Throughout the progression of work on assignments, the teacher will be reflecting upon the choice of work and the performance of the pupil as the work is completed. In practice, the observation of the pupil progress in an individualized pattern of work can make a most significant contribution to the view of the pupil as learner that builds up in the mind of the teacher. The knowledge gleaned at this point will often lead the teacher to modify the plan of work, to intervene where specific help is needed, etc. At the completion of a set of assignments, there can be great value in using some form of test designed to reveal how far the pupil has understood work covered or to reveal specific difficulties. It is on the basis of such tests that the decisions for planning future work are based, but more importantly such tests reveal to the pupils just how well their work is progressing. This demonstration of success and achievement is of the greatest significance if the self esteem of the pupils is to be built up. It is not unrealistic to expect that if the work planned for the pupil was at an appropriate level and if it has been completed effectively, then test marks in the order of 85% plus may become usual.

Continuous assessment

If the routine monitoring described is used to inform a cumulative record of the pupil's progress, then it is quite possible to produce a continuous record of achievement by which the pupil might be assessed. Often the information built up in this continuous record is used to produce a profile of achievement in different aspects of mathematics. This profile is based on the assumption that at this stage it is possible to demonstrate that the pupil is able to succeed in these specific things.

The main criticisms of individualized learning come from a concern that pupils will be isolated from one another as they learn their mathematics, that the system may be abused by teachers who simply accept the soft option and abandon the pupils to work on their own and that learning will take place without an opportunity for pupils to hear or to talk about mathematics. Evidence from the classroom does not support the view that these outcomes are inevitable but it does seem to suggest that working in this way requires a teacher to bring into play an extended range of professional skills to ensure that effective work continues.

Specifically, when working with the least able pupils in this pattern of organization, where the focus is upon the mathematical development of individual pupils, there is real scope for presenting a wide range of mathematical work, but teachers will have to plan so that the range is provided for. The rest of this chapter is, therefore, devoted to producing a list of the sorts of activity which might, as required, find a place in an individual pupil's programme of work. In some cases, the starting point for such an activity might be a suitable piece of published material, a teacher prepared work card, a group investigation, a taped lesson, etc. The list is put forward as a very mixed set of suggestions at all sorts of levels, but hopefully such a list may raise all manner of other possibilities in the mind of the reader.

Practices to encourage the use of language

The onus on the teacher here is to become a listener in the learning situation or to provide someone who is the listener. All comments must be received without criticism or correction if the pupil is to discover that it is the act of verbalizing ideas which is worthy of praise and reward rather than the act of saying *correct* things. In each case, I assume, therefore, that the discussion is used more to reveal the way the pupil thinks and sees things than to direct the pupil to make a single unavoidable observation – the right one!

Describing actions

After an action has taken place, the pupil is invited to describe what he or she has done. Perhaps this is a sorting activity where the pupil describes the 'rules' by which he sorted. It may be a constructional task where something has been made or fitted together where the pupil can describe the relationships between the parts. It may be a description of the way data was collected to produce a graph.

Describing operations

After or during a concrete operation, say a number calculation with cubes, the pupil is invited to describe the operation so that 'stories' to describe operations are built up, e.g., 'If I take three of these and two of these I have five altogether'; 'If I have eight of those, I need two more to make it up to 10'. Quite complicated operations can be described in words which give an opportunity to explore all sorts of relational thinking with language like between, above, in front of, before, after, etc.

Describing objects and patterns

The act of describing objects or pictures can reveal a great deal about the way the pupil observes things. The pupils can be encouraged to refine their descriptions when there is an action taking place as a result of the description. Here, for example, may be two pupils, each looking at a set of objects with many similarities and few differences. One pupil describes one object, the second pupil has to guess which is being described. Sophisticated logic operations can be set up in this way as in the boxed game 'Guess Who' (Milton Bradley) where progressively attributes are eliminated.

Description of this sort stands behind games like Battleships. Simple versions of the same idea can be used where pupil A has a pattern on a grid and pupil B has a blank grid. Pupil A gives instructions to be followed by pupil B who seeks to mark in the same pattern on the blank grid.

Questioning

There is no doubt that the most commonly found pupil/teacher interaction with language is that where teacher poses the question to which the pupil provides the answer. So often, though, questioning seems to be a search for right answers. The teacher receives an answer, rejects it, rephrases the question over and over until they either make the pupil respond automatically with the 'right' answer or even answer it for the pupil by saying 'I hoped you were going to tell me . . .'. This is the most threatening activity for pupils who are unsure of themselves and will either lead to hopeful guessing or noncommittal silence.

It may be far wiser to use questions to which there are no cut and dried answers where the intention is not to test the pupil's accuracy but to explore his perception. Here, questions like 'Which of these shapes do you think you would find hardest to draw?', which requires a valid opinion or judgement to be made, or even inviting comment on the teacher's judgement, hence 'Why do you think I say that would be the hardest one for me to draw?', followed by 'Would you find that the hardest one too?'.

Practices to encourage concrete work

The biggest single factor in giving credibility to concrete work is the acceptance that such work is normal and necessary for anybody enjoying mathematics learning. If work with apparatus is seen as the last resort in compensating for the lack of effectiveness of other more respectable ways of learning mathematics, there is little hope of such work being well received.

The first means of encouraging concrete work must, therefore, be to create a workshop atmosphere in the room where apparatus, models and other mathematical artifacts are seen to be part and parcel of the room. In such an atmosphere, it will be appropriate to encourage such work as:

Making models to represent structure

At the simplest level, this will be as a representation of or as an aid to counting, where, say, the number 3 is represented by three objects. At a complex level, coloured cubes may be used to build up square numbers, rectangular or even cube numbers. Apparatus may be used to build up numbers from tens and units. Reprsentations of a number may be used to demonstrate how many ways it can be made up.

Making models to represent number operations

Building or studying models can be a most valuable way into understanding number operations, not just at the simplest level of representing numbers by objects for the purposde of counting them, but at a more complex level of grouping, partitioning, decomposition in subtraction, place value, base work, etc. In all these and many more the building up of models to represent the calculation can be an ideal preparation for later symbolic reprsentation.

The use of number lines and number tracks opens up a whole further field for exploring relationships between numbers.

Investigating spatial arrays

The development of understanding aspects of shape and space is greatly enriched by experience gained by exploring arrays of dots, peg boards, repeated patterns, symmetrical designs, etc. This can be set up as an investigation where the pupil is given the opportunity to search and observe pre-designed patterns, patterns in nature, etc., in two dimensions. Investigation of three dimensional models, containers, nets of solids, etc., is also an open opportunity for concrete work.

Measurement

In a wide range of units covering all aspects of measurement, there is an opportunity to let the pupil explore with concrete materials and apparatus the progression from the choice of totally arbitrary units, through standard units to universal systems of units.

Representation

Graphs, diagrams, charts and tables are all used at a variety of levels of complexity in mathematics. To start early in

representing information by substituting real objects by concrete objects before the pupil is to lay an appropriate
foundation for later work. Hence building up solid graphs
from cubes, tally charts using matchsticks, bar charts by
sticking coloured squares, etc., are all vital formative experiences. Sorting labels into a table with headed columns or a
Venn diagram or arranging a sequence of events written on
cards into a chain of events joined by arrows can all lead to
an enriched awareness of ways of conveying information.

Practices to encourage discrimination and perception

Many of the low attaining pupils in mathematics whom we
meet at the top of the junior school and in the secondary
school have failed to develop confidence in making perceptions and relating one area of their experience to another. It
can be tempting to feel they never will, and what is certainly
not possible is to pressure them into making connections that
they just cannot see. Surely, the best chance we have is to
expose them to many situations where there is a need to
classify and compare like and unlike attributes. This will
mean an emphasis on simple logic work related to various
aspects of shape, number, symmetry, etc. The tendency is,
however, to supply pupils with examples which all fit the case
we are interested in rather than causing them to discriminate
between examples and non-examples. At all levels it is
possible to include non-examples, but it is seldom done. The
kinds of activity in which this is most easily done include
sorting from mixed examples and non-examples sets by
stated criteria. The sorting can be extended to require justi-
fying certain cases, e.g., 'Why did you leave that one out?',
'Why can I not include that one here?', 'How would the rule
have to change if I put that in there?', etc.

Comparing apparently identical pictures with some things
the same and some different; collecting similar and different
collections of pictures, objects, etc.; prepared sets of cards
with displays of coloured dots or pictures of shapes with
similarities and differences can all provide rich practice for

---

Box 26

Which number from these: 6, 17, 23, 28, 34, 40, fits these facts:

Is the number more than 20?	✓
Can it be made up from fives?	✗
If you add 6, will it end in 0?	✗
Is it an even number?	✓
Do two lots of it make more than 50?	✓

---

sorting in response to such questions as 'What is the same about all these?' or 'Which is the odd one out here?', etc.

Prepared 'enquiry' cards with a set of, say, 5 questions which require a 'Yes' or 'No' answer may be used to promote a classification of objects or pictures to encourage the pupil to decide facts which are true or false about a given object, thereby producing a profile of the object. This sort of activity can then be extended to supplying the profile of answers and the investigation 'For which of these objects would this be the right set of answers?'.

Practice in matching pairs from a wide range of objects and pictures can prove a valuable activity and is easily extended with such structural material as logic blocks to matching objects with one attribute the same but others different, e.g., same shape, different colour, same shape and colour but different size.

Having made discriminations with reference to objects and pictures, there is ample scope to introduce similar work but with the object of the discriminations being numbers. To begin with, dot pictures to represent the numbers may be used, but eventually sets of cards with just numbers written on them will provide a very rich resource. An example of the 'enquiry' card to produce a profile used with numbers is given in Box 26.

Again, it must be stressed that in trying to build up confidence and skill in the pupil, at the level of making discriminations, it is valuable to work at first with comparisons between clear or extreme non-examples and examples. As confidence is built up, it may well be possible to introduce comparisons closer and closer to an example/non-example borderline, where eventually the pupil has really to justify the acceptance of a decision with a logically reasoned case rather than an intuitive assumption.

Practices to encourage problem solving

The forerunner to competent problem solving work in mathematics must be the development of confidence in making decisions and putting forward possible solutions. In this section, therefore, I make just some suggestions which are intended to build up this very confidence.

In this category, a key activity must be causing pupils to take some action or to verbalize their assumptions. Threat should be reduced to a minimum and the consequences of their actions must not be seen as threatening, but they must *do* or *say* something as a result of thinking about what is presented. It may be necessary to use situations which have 100% success as a starting point or which include obvious guessing which is not seen as threatening.

Activities should be designed so that the pupil has to report her or his viewpoint to a third person. If this is too threatening then a recorded comment could be used and self-checking answers supplied.

The activities should be aimed at causing the pupil to respond to the following sorts of enquiry:

Why won't they all fit in?	e.g., objects into a box where some objects are too long, etc.
Why does the pile fall down?	e.g., castle of blocks with some which are the 'wrong' shape
Why won't it go along?	
What have I done wrong?	

There are endless situations that can be contrived with the purpose of causing the pupil to discover what has to be overcome or what is wrong rather than considering how to put it right.

Another whole field of activity which seems well worth exploiting is the 'guessing game'. Such games as Twenty Questions where limited information is given and guesses are made to build up a progressive picture of information. The other guessing situations worth exploiting are not those based on thought and ideas but those based on visual, auditory or other sensory perceptions. Guessing what the photograph is of, or what made this sound, etc.

There is no doubt that these sorts of activity can be most valuable and also lend themselves to a fun aspect which may have great motivational effectiveness, particularly with younger pupils.

The third possible form of activity recommended is that of 'Instruction-giving' which is designed to cause one pupil to interpret information into instructions for another pupil to follow, e.g., describing a configuration of dots displayed before him in words for a partner to interpret and draw onto paper, or giving instructions to a blindfold partner to enable her to cross a room.

It is desirable to move from situations with only one obvious 'cause' to those offering a range of possible 'causes'. The failure to be open to a range of 'possible' suggestions appears to be a common weakness of the less able pupil. Discovery and problem-solving teaching material is often only dealing with a one possible answer situation. The less able problem-solver must be gradually helped to consider and cope with a range of possibilities, any of which may be taken as an acceptable solution.

There is also value in considering activities in which possible solutions are given together with not-possible solutions. The central focus must be that of judging, comparing and evaluating the information. Concern about the manner of recording must not be given too much emphasis. The pupil must not be judged on the basis of skill in communicating but upon observation, discrimination and willingness to compare the possibilities. The onus upon the pupil is to select rather than postulate appropriate solutions.

Specific activities in this category might be some of the following:

Given a tape recorded, spoken, written or illustrated problem or problem situation, pupils are required to select from given alternative solutions which they feel are appropriate.

Given a set of statements about a model, object or picture, the pupil must judge which is false and which is true.

Given a set of solutions and a set of pictures of situations, the pupil is required to match appropriate solution to appropriate picture.

Given a series of pictures, etc., with one missing, the pupil must choose from a given set of possible alternatives which one will 'fit' to make up the set. Some particularly helpful sources of such material are to be found in Samson, Richard W., *The Mind Builder*.[48]

A variety of visual and manipulative puzzles where the 'missing piece' must be selected from a set of possible pieces.

Then, eventually, we come to full problems. In this category the pupil has not only to select possible solutions to problems but has also to postulate the solutions to be considered.

Although it is not always easy to arrange, there are clearly great advantages when the emphasis is on solving 'real' problems. I use the term 'real' in the sense that a solution is not already known to the teacher as being the 'correct' solution. In that the problem needs to be solved before a solution is known, it could be considered real. Solutions to puzzles and 'trick' problems would not in this sense be 'real'. There is no doubt that exposing the less able pupil to such 'pseudo-real' problems normally induces very considerable tension where the pupil feels he is being judged to see if he can 'work out' the 'right' way to do it. Pupils who see such a situation as challenging tend to be highly motivated by the pseudo-real problem – often the less able opt out.

It would be pointless listing endless problems since every teacher is constantly seeing problems arise in the classroom. It is perhaps necessary to stress that the pupils should be encouraged to 'do' this in context rather than 'talking about doing'. 'Go and fix that door back on for me!' is quite different in what it requires of a pupil from answering the question 'What are some of the ways a door can be fixed on?'.

The sorts of activity that lend themselves to this form of active problem-solving include: sorting, unwrapping, packing, untying, constructing, lifting, etc. The ability to solve problems by doing must involve thinking and yet it is so easy to design problem-solving situations that depend solely on thinking without any doing. If we seek to build confidence through success then we must give opportunity for plenty of practice in doing.

It would clearly be unwise to seek to provide encouragement through recognition of success on the one hand, whilst exposing pupils to problems which are likely to prove too difficult by virtue of their content on the other hand. Care must be taken to ensure that the language in which the problem is presented is not beyond that with which the pupil can cope. If solving a problem depends heavily on factual information that is not possessed by pupils, we must either enable them to learn or recall it before the problem is presented or give the information to them in forms which they can use.

Practices to give opportunity to enjoy aesthetic experiences

So very often the work produced by the least able lacks not only in accuracy but also in neatness. After a while, many pupils become convinced of the unacceptability of their own work on the basis of appearance alone. Whether this is the adverse consequence of the endeavours of successive teachers to encourage pupils to produce model work by displaying only fine, neat and attractive examples on classroom walls, does not perhaps matter. I have noted, however, that the impact of producing really attractive work on pupils whose work is generally indifferent and whose confidence is low, can be quite remarkable.

We are in danger of assuming that certain basic skills are present which just are not. I have suggested activities here related to certain problems which I have noticed with many pupils.

Problems with location

The drawing of a line accurately between two points is a skill which may need practice. Some pupils start only approximately at a given point and draw in the general direction of the second point, rather than actually locating accurately the two points. Lots of practice with dog to dot pictures may be needed here. Practice at drawing accurate triangles by first drawing three dots and then joining them exactly is also valuable. Progressing from dot outlines to shapes can then enable pupils to produce very accurate hexagons and other pleasing shapes just by joining dots. It cannot be supposed that a great deal of spatial awareness will yet have developed for the pupil who feels himself to be 'just joining the dots', but the feeling of achievement associated with producing quite ambitious shapes accurately and the aesthetic pleasure it brings is worthwhile enough.

Problems with copying accurately

It is easy to assume that pupils can analyse the construction of a pattern accurately enough to copy it. All teachers are aware of pupils who, in their endeavour to copy something, spend the major part of their time rubbing out failed attempts. I believe, to start with, we are far wiser to help pupils to build up from simple to more complex patterns by adding, perhaps, one line at a time, rather than expecting them to copy a finished pattern. So, for example, many pupils who would be quite unable to attempt the task of drawing the pattern shown in Diagram 10a might produce an exceed-

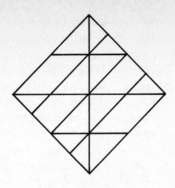

Diagram 10(a)

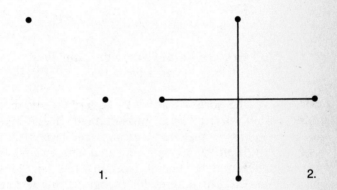

1. 2.

Diagram 10(b)

ingly pleasing copy if asked to do it in stages as in Diagram
10b.

Problems with circles

So many attempts to use a pair of compasses end up in
abortive frustration. Admittedly, the nature of school compasses is the main contributory factor, but if we are really
honest the level of manipulative skill required to produce

pleasing and accurate circles is really quite high. I have found it is so much less frustrating and, in a strange way, so much more powerful, when pupils are given a card strip with which to produce circles. A strip with a pinhole and pencil hole at a fixed distance apart is all that is required. I have found many pupils absolutely fascinated when they discover that any odd shaped piece of card with a pinhole and a pencil hole will also produce a circle when rotated.

Having pinned a card to paper also presents the possibility of drawing round a template in successive rotated positions to produce most intriguing rotating patterns, which when coloured can be really beautiful.

It is this discovery that beautiful work can actually be produced so simply that so often opens a floodgate of motivation for those pupils who feel they cannot do beautiful work.

Problems of repeating the same thing twice

Because of the sorts of difficulty described and because of difficulties associated with measurement, it can be exacting for some pupils to produce a second shape identical to a first one drawn. If any work with repeated patterns, tessellations, etc., is to be done, the benefit from making templates cannot be over stated. All manner of intriguing shape and design work can be set up using templates, which may well lead into the beginnings of three dimensional representation. it is not a great step from a to b as shown in Diagram 11.

These are just a few of the points at which it is comparatively easy to help pupils from dismay and frustration to pleasure and fulfillment. I have witnessed many low attaining secondary pupils whose mathematics work generally began to take on a new impetus altogether once they had discovered how pleasing could be the look of their work. Some would argue that it was a form of spoon feeding that is being advocated and that by removing the challenge of 'getting to grips with compasses properly', we make the pupils more dependent and less likely to develop their skills. By providing

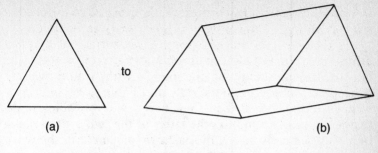

to

(a)   (b)

Diagram 11

a coping strategy, we are denying the pupils the opportunity to solve problems properly.

It is interesting that this should seem so clear an issue over the presentation of spatial work, but in fact it runs right across the whole field of learning for these pupils. It is also the most significant philosophical watershed when approaching the teaching of the low attaining pupils. Let us then focus on the issue as it seems to arise so naturally out of this discussion of how to help the pupils.

Some would say it is not helpful to simplify complex fields of knowledge by breaking them down into small steps, since the pupils will then learn as unrelated and separate things which are highly interrelated and complex. In mathematics, this argument would be applied both to the concepts presented in mathematics and the language in which they are presented.

By analogy – if you teach a child to walk by using crutches he will never be able to learn what real independent walking is about and, therefore, rather than helping his development, you are hindering it.

Others will argue that unless we simplify and break down complex fields of knowledge into steps which learners perceive to be manageable, then they are not likely to sustain any effort or interest in learning once feelings of failure become dominant. But that once small successes are experienced, then the motivation and interest generated is likely to lead to further learning.

The analogy there is that such enjoyment can be gained

from walking that it is worth enabling the child to experience it by providing whatever support is necessary at the time.

My own view is that in adopting the former of the two attitudes, we may be presenting a most attractive argument but be leaving many of the pupils with whom we are concerned floundering hopelessly and liable to become confirmed in the belief that they never will be able to do mathematics. By adopting the latter of the two attitudes, we may well see early and enthusiastic involvement in the work that is put before the pupils. We must take heed, though, that we do continually stretch the pupils and plan work in such a way that the new found confidence of learners causes them to cast away the crutches.

Finally, we cannot leave consideration of 'how' without raising the broader issues related to organization of the work within the school. The organization of the mathematics work for the least able in a secondary school has to be seen in relation to the organization of the mathematics work for the rest of the pupils and also in relation to the curriculum policy of the whole school.

The approach to individualized work described in the previous chapter may well constitute no mismatch at all with the mainstream of the mathematics department if there is an individualized approach in operation throughout. If this is the case, the decision which will have to be made is whether the least able are to be withdrawn into a separate group or integrated into mixed ability groups.

Theoretically, neither will pose a different problem, though in practice there do seem to be advantages where the least able can be organized into a smaller group. The advantage of this is so often offset by the feeling that this is a low priority group. Whether in the mixed ability group or separate, the work, if effectively planned, should lead to a high level of success and associated high self esteem.

In many situations, however, the work for the low attaining pupils is quite separately planned from the mainstream. Individualized work applied in that situation is likely to be aimed at covering different mathematics from the start, with class taught or class paced work in the mainstream. The problem that is likely to arise here is that transfer from a special group, where success at an individual level has been very high, back into the mainstream becomes less easy as time goes on.

Where there is this mismatch between philosophies behind the mainstream and the low attainers work, it is essential to plan work for a pupil very carefully before integration into the mainstream. It may even be necessary to plan a special link course between the two where the choice of assignments for the individual pupil is affected more by the mathematical 'destination' than by any other considerations at that transition stage.

Often a bigger concern than that of integration back into the mainstream is the problem of mismatch between assessment models in use. The norm referenced examination type assessment, where all pupils do the same questions and get marks ranked in order, may be used in the mainstream of the school. For pupils who have been exposed only to tests designed to reveal the level at which they were being highly successful, there is clearly a crisis. Many schools have overcome this problem by designing a graduated set of tests with pupils able to work at that part of the range on which their marks remain high. Such a procedure of linking tests is then used across the ability range and a rank order produced on the basis of the marks and the level of the test.

In some schools where individualized work is organized from a hierarchically arranged material bank, a continuous assessment procedure can be used based upon the level at which each pupil is ordinarily working.

Whatever arrangement is used, it is essential that any mismatch between the syllabus or assessment for the mainstream and the low attainers is openly discussed and allowed for by teachers in both parts of the school.

The work must also be seen in relation to the whole policy for the school. It may be necessary to negotiate over the provision of apparatus and suitable workshop rooms for the least able. The pattern of timetabling may not be determined by the mathematics department but dictated right across the school. Where the balance of single and double periods is inappropriate, the intended pattern of work may well have to be modified or the timetabling challenged.

In general, though, the work provided is likely to be most effective in school if the philosophy and rationale, once developed, is understood by colleagues and, even if not agreed with, is at least allowed for in the way that the work is set up and resources are allocated in the school. Sadly, there is all too often nobody in the decision-making hierarchy of the school who carries responsibility or a major concern for the work of these least prestigious pupils.

seven

The Special Needs of the Older Pupil

For one reason or another the mathematics work, and work in other subjects also, provided for pupils in the last two years of schooling is often seen as needing to be different from that previously encountered by the least able pupils. A full discussion of why this is so and whether it is reasonable is not the subject of this chapter. Instead, I shall proceed on the assumption that a decision has been made to plan a different approach to the content at the top of the secondary school.

The significant assumption operating here would appear to be that pupils at this stage are now closer to entering the 'real world' than they have been previously. However much we may wish the pupils to realize the significance of this it is all too often the case that the pupil has no real idea where they will fit into the world of work or even if they *will* fit into it. There may seem to be sense in trying to argue that 'when you start you will need to know some mathematics'. It may even be tempting to try to argue that 'if you can learn these mathematical facts and techniques you will be 'more likely to get a good job'. Even if the pupils were to be convinced by such utilitarian arguments it is unlikely that the pupils will even be enterered for C.S.E. and so they are demonstrably not true. It would seem far more worthwhile, if a special course is to be provided, to use as a starting point what the pupil knows and seek to give opportunities to apply it in real situations.

Traditionally, courses where application of mathematics is involved have been planned on the basis of questions like these:

(a) What mathematical topic shall we encourage the pupil to apply?
(b) In what real life situations do we find this topic used?
(c) How can we plan or simulate experience of that situation so that the right mathematics is applied?

Hence with that sort of emphasis on the mathematics topic to be covered, say percentages, we try to find examples of practical situations where they will be used. Hence:

	Bank Interest
Maths Area	Hire Purchase
e.g. Percentages	Statistical Surveys
	Taxation

I shall call this 'Type 1 Topic Work'.

Another approach altogether could be taken if first we consider a real job which can be done. In engaging the pupil in doing the job we are aware that there will be all sorts of demands on the pupil which will cause many mathematics skills to be used. For example a job such as building a small wall may be identified. A range of mathematical skills would have been brought into play. Let us call this a Type 2 approach.

There is no doubt that the easier of the two approaches to plan is type 1. There is no doubt that the approach which comes to teachers' minds most readily is type 1. There is no doubt that the approach in which it is most easy to control the mathematics is type 1. But there is no doubt that the approach which is most like the real world is type 2 where the reason for doing the job is that it needs to be done, not that it gives the 'right' mathematical experience. In addition, to this there are three aspects of the type 1 approach which are liable, even guaranteed, to produce particular problems for pupils who are low in self-esteem and low therefore in confidence. Some of these are listed.

1. The emphasis on the mathematics of the topic requires that the pupils have a facility in mathematics at the level required, can recall the appropriate mathematics accurately and can relate it to the practical situation.

2. So often the end product of the topic work is an appropriate mathematically stated solution, conclusion drawn, comparison made or data presented in a particular mathematical way. The focus is therefore on doing 'the right mathematics' rather than completing the 'job', i.e. the focus is on outcome rather than process.

3. So often the ability of the pupil to see what happens is far more advanced than the ability to appreciate why this has happened or to realize the significance of it. The drawing of conclusions is therefore fraught with difficulties which are of a different order from those encountered in gathering data.

Teachers who have sought to work with the type 2 topic work with older pupils are not numerous in schools. Often they apologise because it does not 'seem to be real maths work' that they are engaged in but their reason for continuing with it is that the pupils enter into the work in a completely different way.

I shall endeavour to outline therefore some of the salient points worth considering at the planning stage for teachers who begin to provide opportunity for some of the mathematics time for older pupils to be taken up in this way:

(a) Pupils must become actively involved in doing from the start rather than in planning to do. There is a vast difference between planning what could be the cost of buying food for a hypothetical family and actually entering the supermarket to make the purchases.

(b) There is a great need for something tangible to be produced or impact of the work to be seen from the earliest possible moment of the work. (See Box 27)

(c) The span of interest is likely to be short. There is little hope of re-kindling enthusiasm after motivation has gone. So often the motivation breaks down following frustration when materials are not available, the desired effect is not produced and things start to go wrong. In the first place it is probably wise to have short term objectives which once achieved can always easily be extended if appropriate. On the other hand it is almost impossible to

---

BOX 27

In one school I visited some fifth year pupils who had produced cards for a word game that they had devised to help pupils to learn to read. Quite apart from the mathematics involved in the cutting of the cards, planning sets of words, applying letraset etc., there was a real sense of pleasure that they created something really useful. The topic became really fulfilling when they saw the cards actually in use lower down in the school.

---

keep up the momentum if the objectives are beyond reach. It may even become necessary to abandon the topic, salvaging what we can if motivation has been lost which in itself is likely to have an adverse effect on the pupils' willingness to be involved in future.

(d) Encouragement in what has been achieved is vital and is likely to lead to further success. It is so easy and tempting to criticize and compare the work produced with some expected standard with the hope that that will make the pupil 'get it right'. This may well do great harm to self-esteem and lead to non-cooperation and breakdown in the work. It may seem that by holding up and praising the work of the pupil as 'just the sort of thing we wanted', we will encourage others but by implication they may read our action as saying 'your work is just what we did not want to see'. When we start to encourage self-evaluation and criticism of a pupil's own work and when we are seen to encourage the hard-working and honest endeavour of the pupil we start to create an atmosphere in which self-esteem can be built up.

It is clear that the purely mathematical outcomes and benefits derived from doing a particular type 2, job-based topic will be far less easy to specify. Clearly it will be affected, not only by the range of mathematical questions raised during the completion of the job, but also by the repertoire of mathematical skills on which the pupil is able to draw. Another significant factor will be the extent to which the teacher feels able, has time or is willing to enter into discussion about the mathematical problems being encountered. Nevertheless in the absence of such discussion it is probable that a great deal of mathematical thinking has gone on in the mind of the pupil.

It can be hard, sometimes, to convince teachers that the really significant activity, mathematically speaking, happened as the pupil indulged in the mathematical thinking. For example in the experience of Box 27 the moment for the pupil which may have been absolutely paramount in its significance could have been when in his mind he resolved the problem – 'How can I use the gauge on the guillotine to ensure that all the cards are exactly the same size?' Hence the moment of solving that may have been sufficient justification in itself for doing the activity. So often the teacher would feel that the significant activity would be writing up of the experience so that there was 'something to show' for all that work.

Ideally job-based topics need not only be contained within the confines of the maths area or even the school. (Box 28). But it is bound to raise problems and issues within the school once the base of the work broadens. The three likely areas of pressure will be the cost of resourcing this work (Box 29), pressures within the timetabling arrangements for the school and potential conflicts with colleagues. The problems with colleagues do not arise only because of crossing conventional subject boundaries but also because of resistance to the way of working. This resistance is sometimes based upon concern that a group of pupils, which may contain a number who are considered to be 'trouble makers', are allowed a measure of freedom which is not felt by some to be deserved and may even be perceived as a 'reward' for wrong doers.

It may well be the case that the senior secondary pupils with whom this work is being done are those who have been experiencing repeated failure. In consequence they may well also be disaffected towards mathematics. For many such pupils this type 2 approach can provide a new horizon but for some reason it is difficult to find acceptance for such a radical

---

BOX 28

In a residential ESN (M) boys' school I have seen really impressive applications of mathematics and of life skills in an ambitious out of school journey with tasks to achieve on the way. Each pupil has their own specific planned journey to make with a timetable to be adhered to, specific check-in points in town with a rendez-vous to be made, specific items to purchase, a package to post etc.

BOX 29

In one school a group of low ability pupils were given the opportunity to build a greenhouse using second-hand materials, which were available at very little cost and paid for by a loan from the school fund. The building exercise was mathematically exceedingly rich. The resultant building, though thoroughly unconventional was none the less serviceable and of course the object of great pride for the group who built it. A subsequent group of pupils raised from seed and brought on tomato plants whose produce was sold off. Accounts were kept and before long the loan was paid off and profits made. In a third phase the profit has been re-invested in compost, seed, etc. and a wide variety of bedding plants brought on and sold.

---

idea. The overriding fear seems to be that pupils who are in any case difficult to handle might become totally unmanageable in a situation which is designed to allow them a great deal of freedom in their activity. It has to be said that such comments are found as points of criticism from those who have not ever sought to work in this way far more commonly than as points of concern by those who have.

The potential for this type 2 approach must not, however, be seen only as an expedient way of working for disaffected pupils. It could be seen as a high level activity which could give new meaning for all pupils at this stage in their schooling and, with a growing tendency towards moving out from school into the community, it is becoming more practicable. Some suggested activities worth considering for job based topic work are: Making, Designing, Planning, Decorating, Film making, Dismantling, Repairing, Spending etc. In each of these categories there may be many activities that suggest themselves.

What matters is that we recognize that our justification for the topic work is that mathematics is applied. It is not that the pupil is required to 'write up' a detailed account of what was done or that once the job is over the teacher goes back and draws out all the mathematics from it.

Clearly such topic work would cease to be of value or interest if this was all the mathematics the pupil was engaged in, nor is it likely that such work could be accommodated within an examination course. But this broader view of application of mathematics to real life situations has great relevance when we are honest in considering the needs of older pupils.

eight

Assessment

I have already touched upon assessment procedures in a previous chapter but it seems important finally to consider assessment principles in the light of my preceding argument. Further it is worthwhile considering what we are trying to discover about the pupils and also whether what we discover has broader implications for the teacher or even for the mathematics department or the school.

First then some key questions:

Is the purpose of the assessment to reveal information about the pupil's own personal mathematical development, or to provide information relative to the other pupils in the group?

Will the fact that information has been gained by the assessment procedure lead to any change in what the pupil is actually required to do in the mathematics lesson?

Is it intended that the assessment procedure should reveal what the pupil is able to do, or to identify what the pupil is not able to do?

Will the assessments made have any part to paly in monitoring the effectiveness of the teacher in planning and providing for the mathematics learning of the pupil being assessed?

The alternative to raising these and other penetrating questions would seem to be to allow assessment to be a mindless and meaningless task which is at worst a total waste of time and at best a well-intentioned but lost opportunity. In the Schools Council Working Paper 72, Low Attainers in Mathematics 5–16[49]: Policies and Practices in Schools, the authors claim:

> The value of assessment lies in the use which is made of the information it reveals. It is, therefore, of permanent importance to decide why the assessment is to be made and then to consider in the light of this information what adjustments should be made to the organisations, courses or teaching approaches.

The Cockcroft Report,[50] Mathematics Counts, makes the assertion that:

> Testing, whether written, oral or practical, should never be an end in itself but should be a means of providing information which can form the basis of future action.

In short, it may be better not to assess at all than to assess and take nfo notice of what is being revealed.

There is then a case for considering:

(a) What purposes might assessment serve?
(b) When might assessment be done?
(c) How might assessment be carried out?
(d) What are the principal difficulties in assessment?

Each is discussed in more detail below, although clearly what is ideal in one situation might be quite unhelpful in another. In an attempt at clarity of presentation and for ease of reference the headings (a), (b) and (c) are dealt with in the form of a table (see Table 1), whilst (d) is the subject of a discussion and examples.

For the sake of reference I will classify forms of assessment by applying the following statements:

1. The principal objective is to compare the pupils' ability or performance in mathematics with that of other pupils. For purposes of later reference assessment procedures designed to meet this need will be called Type 1.

Table 1

	(a) What purposes might assessment serve?	(b) When might assessment be done?	(c) How might assessment be carried out?
Type 1	Producing rank orders. Aid to setting/grouping. Screening to identify pupils worth closer observation, and diagnosis at both ends of ability range.	At any time across a group of pupils.	Formal examination or test situation for whole group. Allocation of marks on scale for routine marking of classwork and homework.
Type 2	Diagnosis of weakness. Information for planning remedial action.	After previous screening or referral has indicated need for diagnostic testing.	Formal testing individually. Informal testing individually. Analysis of routine marking of classwork and homework.
Type 3	Monitoring progress and achievement. Information for planning future work. Evaluation of usefulness of work given.	After previous screening or referral has indicated need for diagnostic testing. Regularly on completion of sections of work.	Formal testing individually. Informal testing individually. Observations of pupil.
Type 4	To provide background information for course planning. Evaluation of impact of work upon pupil.	Continuously as pupil works at mathematics.	Observation of pupil. Informal testing. Completion of check lists.

2. The principal objective is to identify areas of mis-understanding, weakness or failure in mathematics. (For later reference – Type 2.)
3. The principal objective is to assess whether mathematics previously encountered has been understood. (For later reference – Type 3.)
4. The principal objective is to reveal other facets of the pupil's development which might have some bearing upon his/her performance in mathematics learning. (For later reference – Type 4.)

Thus follows Table 1.

It is worth observing that historically Type 1 assessment has been very common and in some schools the only form of assessment ever deliberately in use, in some form or another, ranging from formal external public examinations, end of year examinations, down to the weekly collection of homework marks. Type 2 assessment tends to be used quite commonly after it has become clear that a pupil is making no progress with what is being presented to him/her. Tests may be used as a means of pinpointing specific areas of weakness. Type 3 assessment is at present rare in schools, and is usually informal. The significant exception to this is in those mathematics schemes such as the Kent Mathematics Project[51] and SMILE Project[52] where in both cases an individualized approach to learning incorporates regular monitoring of pupil progress which in turn influences the teacher's subsequent choice of work for each pupil. A similar judgement is often assumed to be happening when in an intuitive way the teacher decides when to move on to the next topic or part of the syllabus. It is arguable that in practice the failure to monitor successful learning and achievement on the part of each individual pupil is the most significant contributory factor to the failure of some pupils. Such failure is most evident where whole classes are taught the same thing at the same time, and the judgement of when to leave one topic and move to another is based on the asumption that the work is now understood by all the pupils. The fact that partial

---

Box 30

The following excerpt is taken from an Article by J. Maxwell from the Community Education and Arts Project writing about her observations on why people fail to learn. ('Mathematics in School', 1983 May.)

One of the adult students said that her problems with mathematics had arisen from a lack of opportunity to catch up if she was absent or had failed to understand in class – everything had moved too fast – and left her behind. Her nine-year-old daughter is now suffering from the reverse – she finds mathematics too easy and is bored and frustrated.

---

understanding, or even in some cases total confusion, exists in the minds of a few pupils is hidden or ignored (Box 30). The cumulative effect of such failure is absolutely crucial for some pupils. If in practice there is substance in this argument, then it must be conceded that, at the other end of the ability range, there could well be cumulative effects for the able pupil who is constantly working well within the limits of his or her ability and therefore underachieving.

Type 4 assessment procedures may be little more than matters of casual observation on the part of teachers, often randomly made and seldom recorded in any systematic way. The significance of some of the information available through Type 4 assessment cannot be overstated. It will include such aspects as: 'Can the pupil read the text in which the mathematics is presented?' 'Is there evidence of specific visual, auditory or psycho-motor problems?' etc. Such things though casually observed must not surely be casually treated. In order to encourage deliberate efforts to make such observations the Classroom Observation Procedure (COP)[53] has been developed in ILEA, but such a procedure is likely to prove more lengthy than is realistic for ordinary use in schools except with individual pupils for whom special concern exists.

(d) The principal difficulties

The five major problems in practice are seen to be:

1. Selecting the appropriate assessment material.
2. Finding the time to carry out assessment.
3. Interpreting the results and keeping records.
4. Making use of the information gained.
5. Concern about the effects of testing upon the pupils.

1. I have attempted to clarify criteria for selecting appropriate assessment material. Hopefully this will have made such selection easier and more effective. There is, however, no substitute for looking at materials. A school collection of assessment material is to be recommended, with samples of published tests available. County Advisers, School Psychological Services, Teachers' Centres, Mathematics Centres, etc., may all have inspection material available. Publishers' brochures, exhibitions, and specialist journals are worth scouring for ideas. Not to be overlooked either is the possibility that home produced materials might be of great value and may, as in Type 4 assessment, be almost the only source of material.

   If home produced materials are to be developed, it is surely worth discussing them with colleagues, sharing them, modifying them in the light of experience as they are used, and then keeping them for future use in a way that they are easily retrieved. This may involve careful indexing or even production of a suitable computer retrieval system.

2. Finding time to test is perhaps the greatest problem expressed by teachers. Clearly Type 1 assessments are the easiest to administer since they involve a formal 'examination' type approach where all pupils are involved at once for the same fixed period of time, with the teacher minimally involved in the testing. It is the more individual focus in Type 2, Type 3 and Type 4, which is likely to involve the teacher much more closely, that has the greatest value in planning pupils' subsequent work. Easy

solutions are hard to find but the following seem to prove useful in some schools:

(i) As a special event co-operative use of two teachers in some schools creates an 'extra' person being available to administer tests. This 'extra' may be a person with remedial expertise, used as a 'consultant' as needed for testing pupils. It may be a willing member of staff with non-teaching time who can be called on – an ideal opportunity for a Head of Mathematics to develop a supporting role for colleagues in the Department. In the primary school it can be less easy but many Heads co-operate in this way. It may be well worth exploring the possibilities of this kind. In practice it may mean no more than arranging a floating member of staff for a few days in a year.

(ii) Planned testing as a regular part of pupils' work is practised in some schools to cover Type 2 and particularly Type 3.

For this purpose schools often use test material selected from a set of criterion referenced tests, e.g., Yardsticks,[54] Somerset Assessment in Mathematics,[55] etc. The important thing is that the testing is part of the usual routine rather than a special event. Where it is intended to monitor individual progress such a practice, coupled with effective record keeping, is invaluable. It is important that such tests are seen by the pupils as a real opportunity to demonstrate just how well they are doing. Therefore regular tests must match the work the pupils have actually done, giving a high chance of success in most of the test. Teachers who use regular testing in this way argue that the 'loss' of learning time given over to testing is more than repaid by the greater effectiveness of planning future work, and identifying precise areas for remedial action.

There is always the very real danger, however, of conveying to the pupils that only what is tested is important. Once this attitude is expressed by the pupils it may well undermine all attempts to encourage anything but a cynical attitude towards mathematics.

3. In selecting appropriate tests the whole method of obtaining and recording results must be considered. In general,

the simpler the system the more likely it is that teachers will find it useful. Lists of marks and single rank orders may be adequate for planning sets across a year group, but where there is interest in individual pupils they are nowhere near as useful as visually interpreted profiles, charts, etc. The tests and recording procedure must clarify and highlight areas of strength or weakness. In general, this is most likely to happen where the assessment instrument is in some way matched to the 'concept framework' or 'hierarchy of mathematics' against which the mathematics learning is planned. Actually, testing is considerably more valuable than simply recording check lists of what has been given to the pupils to do. As a cautionary note, it must be said that assessment used to monitor individual pupils' progress and produce profiles of 'successful learning' is likely to reveal weaknesses not only in the learning but also in the teaching, particularly where the logical progression in the work is poorly matched to the development of mathematical thinking of the pupils. It has to be said that many planned syllabi in use in schools have whole sections which really do not stand up to close scrutiny in the light of information gained from 'poor test results' of pupils.

4. The question of making use of information is not easy because the constraints which exist for a teacher may seem to rule out of order certain questions. For example:

> *What is the teacher to do whose testing seems to indicate that the school syllabus requirement is quite wrong for this or that pupil?*

> *The pupil may appear to need concrete materials that are not available to the Department.*

> *A fundamental question might be raised over the policy on grouping pupils in the school.*

> *A need might be demonstrated for specialist support or referral which is not usually available in the school.*

If there is value in assessing pupils' needs then teachers must be prepared to negotiate on the basis of what they discover even if this does mean challenging the received view in their school.

References

1. Cockcroft, W., *Mathematics Counts,* H.M.S.O. 1982.
2. Committee of Enquiry. Special Educational Needs. Report of the Committee of Enquiry into the Education of Handicapped Children and Young People. Chairman Mrs. H.M. Warnock, London, H.M.S.O., 1978.
3. Buxton, L, *Do You Panic About Maths?* London, Heinemann Educational Books, 1981.
4. Rutter, M. *et al., Fifteen Thousand Hours: Secondary Schools and their Effects on Children,* London, Open Books, 1979.
5. Maslow, A.H., *Motivation and Personality,* New York, Harper Bros, 1954.
6. Cockcroft, W., *Mathematics Counts.*
7. SMILE project I.L.E.A.
8. Kent Mathematics Project Kent L.E.A., Ward Lock Educational, 1979.
9. Hulicka, I.M., in Roucek, J.S. (ed.), *The Slow Learner,* London, Peter Owen, 1969.
10. Williams, P., in Varma, V.P. (ed.), *Stress In Children,* University of London Press, 1973.
11. Gulliford, R., in Weddell, K. and Raybould, E.C. (eds) 'The Early Identification of Educationally "at risk" Children', Educational Review, University of Birmingham, 1976.
12. Chazan, M. in Weddell, K. and Raybould, E.C. (eds) 'The Early Identification of Educationally "at risk" children'.
13. Holt, J., *How Children Fail,* London, Pitman, 1964.
14. Denscombe, M. in Woods, P., *Pupil Strategies,* London, Croom Helm, 1980.
15. Donaldson, M. *Childrens' Minds,* London, Fontana, 1978.
16. Assessment of Performance Unit-Mathematical Development Surveys, Foxman, D.D. *et al,* H.M.S.O.
17. C.S.M.S. details in Hart, K.M. (ed.) *Childrens' Understanding of Mathematics 11–16,* London, John Murray, 1981.

18. Skemp, R., *The Psychology of Learning Mathematics*, Harmondsworth, Penguin, 1971.
19. Markle, S.M. and Tiemann, W.L., *Really Understanding Concepts*, Champaign Illinois, Stipes Publishing Co. 1969.
20. Barnes, D. *et al*, *Language, the Learner and School*, Harmondsworth, Penguin Books, 1969.
21. Piaget, J., *The Child's Conception of Number*, London, Routledge Kegan Paul, 1952.
22. Dawson, S. and Trivett, J. in Floyd, A. (ed.), *Developing Mathematical Thinking*, for Open University by Addison Wesley 1981.
23. Lovatt, M., article in Special Education: Forward Trends, Sept. 1972.
24. Kagan, J., 'Impulsive and Reflective Children: Significance of Conceptual Tempo', in Krumboltz, J.D. (ed.), *Learning and The Educational Process*, Chicago, Rand McNally, 1964.
25. Combs, A.W. and Syngg, D., *Individual Behaviour, a Perceptual Approach to Behaviour*, New York, Harper & Bros, 1959.
26. Stones, E., *An Introduction To Educational Psychology*, London, University Paper Backs, 1966.
27. Kogan, N. and Wallach, M.A., *Risk Taking*, New York, Holt, Reinhart and Winston, 1964.
28. Klausmeier, H.J. and Loughlin, L.J., 'Behaviour During Problem Solving Among Children of Low, Average and High Intelligence', Journal of Educ. Psychology 52: 148–52, 1961.
29. De Cecco, J.P., *The Psychology of Language Thought and Instruction*, New York, Holt, Reinhart and Winston, 1969.
30. Peel, E.A., *The Pupil's Thinking*, London, Oldbourne Book Co., 1960.
31. Garry, R. and Kingsley, H.L., *The Nature and Conditions of Learning*, Englewood City, New Jersey, Prentice Hall Inc., 1970.
32. Bruner, J.S., *Towards a Theory of Instruction*, Cambridge Mass., The Belknap Press of Harvard University Press, 1971.
33. Bogoiavlenski, D.N. and Menchinskaia, N.A., in Simon, B. and Simon, J., *Educational Psychology in the U.S.S.R.*, London, Routledge Kegan Paul, 1963.
34. Duncker, K., *The Psychology of Productive (Creative) Thinking*, Translated from German in Matyushkin, A.M. (ed.), *The Psychology of Thinking*, Moscow, Progress, 1965.
35. Lindsey, P.H. and Norman, D.A., *Human Information Processing*, New York, Academic Press, 1972.
36. Burton, L., *The Three M's*, Mathematical Education for Teaching Vol. 3 No. 1 July 1977.
37. Gagné, R.M., *The Conditions of Learning*, New York, Holt, Reinhart and Winston, 1965.
38. Rohwer, W.D., Ammon, P.E. and Cramer, P., *Understanding Intellectual Development – Three Approaches to Theory and Practice*, Hinsdale, Illinois, Dryden, 1974.
39. Bruner, J., *Towards a Theory of Instruction*, Cambridge, Mass., Belknapp, 1966.

40. Schroder, H.M. and Hunt, D.E., 'Failure Avoidance in Situational Interpretation and Problem Solving', Psychological Monographs Vol. 71 No. 33, 1957.
41. Nichols, S.L., Nichols, K.A. and Burden, R.L., 'The Relationship Between Self Evaluation and Reading Progress: Some Paradoxical Findings', Remedial Educational Vol. 12 No. 4, Nov. 1977.
42. Gagné, R.M. and Smith, E.C., 'A Study of the Effects of Verbalization on Problem Solving', Journal of Educational Psychology Vol. 63 No. 1, 1962.
43. Samson, R.W., *The Mind Builder*, New York, E.P. Dutton & Co. Inc., 1965.
44. Peel, E.A., *The Pupil's Thinking*, London, Oldbourne Book Co., 1960.
45. Dyson, A., *Giants and Pygmies: an Approach to Mathematics with Less Able Students in a Secondary School*, Mathematics in School May 83, Longman.
46. Beard, R., *Teaching and Learning in Higher Education*, Harmondsworth, Penguin, 1970.
47. Graves, D.H., *Writing: teachers and children at work*, London, Heinemann, 1983.
48. Samson, Richard W., *The Mind Builder*, New York, E.P. Dutton and Co., 1965.
49. Schools Council Working Paper 72, Denvir B., Stolz C. and Brown, M., 'Low Attainers in Mathematics 5–16 Policies and Practices in Schools', Methuen Educational 1982.
50. Cockcroft, W., *Mathematics Coiunts*, H.M.S.O., 1982.
51. Kent Mathematics Project, Kent L.E.A., Ward Lock Educational, 1979.
52. SMILE Project, I.L.E.A.
53. Classroom Observation Procedure, I.L.E.A. Schools Psychological Service 1977 – Details from Hoxton House, 34 Hoxton St., London N1.
54. Yardsticks, Criterion Referenced Tests in Mathematics, Nelson, 1975.
55. Somerset Assessment in Mathematics. Globe Education/Macmillan Education, 1981.

Index